Making Change in Complex Organizations

Also available from ASQ Quality Press:

The Strategic Knowledge Management Handbook: Driving Business Results by Making Tacit Knowledge Explicit
Arun Hariharan

Failure Mode and Effects Analysis (FMEA) for Small Business Owners and Non-Engineers: Determining and Preventing What Can Go Wrong
Marcia M. Weeden

The Quality Toolbox, Second Edition
Nancy R. Tague

Root Cause Analysis: Simplified Tools and Techniques, Second Edition
Bjørn Andersen and Tom Fagerhaug

The Certified Six Sigma Green Belt Handbook, Second Edition
Roderick A. Munro, Govindarajan Ramu, and Daniel J. Zrymiak

The Certified Manager of Quality/Organizational Excellence Handbook, Fourth Edition
Russell T. Westcott, editor

The Certified Six Sigma Black Belt Handbook, Second Edition
T.M. Kubiak and Donald W. Benbow

The ASQ Auditing Handbook, Fourth Edition
J.P. Russell, editor

The ASQ Quality Improvement Pocket Guide: Basic History, Concepts, Tools, and Relationships
Grace L. Duffy, editor

To request a complimentary catalog of ASQ Quality Press publications, call 800-248-1946, or visit our Web site at http://www.asq.org/quality-press.

Making Change
in Complex
Organizations

George K. Strodtbeck, III

ASQ Quality Press
Milwaukee, Wisconsin

American Society for Quality, Quality Press, Milwaukee, WI 53203
© 2016 by ASQ
All rights reserved. Published 2016.
Printed in the United States of America.

22   21   20   19   18   17   16   5   4   3   2   1

Library of Congress Cataloging-in-Publication Data

Names: Strodtbeck, George K., 1954- author.
Title: Making change in complex organizations / George K. Strodtbeck, III.
Description: First Edition. | Milwaukee, WI : American Society for
Quality, Quality Press, 2016.
Identifiers: LCCN 2016005439 | ISBN 9780873899284 (hardcover : alk. paper)
Subjects: LCSH: Organizational change. | Communication in organizations. |
  Corporate culture.
Classification: LCC HD58.8 .S787 2016 | DDC 658.4/06—dc23
LC record available at http://lccn.loc.gov/2016005439

Publisher: Seiche Sanders
Acquisitions Editor: Matt T. Meinholz
Managing Editor: Paul Daniel O'Mara
Production Administrator: Randall Benson

ASQ Mission: The American Society for Quality advances individual,
organizational, and community excellence worldwide through learning, quality
improvement, and knowledge exchange.

Attention Bookstores, Wholesalers, Schools, and Corporations: ASQ Quality
Press books, video, audio, and software are available at quantity discounts with
bulk purchases for business, educational, or instructional use. For information,
please contact ASQ Quality Press at 800-248-1946, or write to ASQ Quality Press,
P.O. Box 3005, Milwaukee, WI 53201-3005.

To place orders or to request ASQ membership information, call 800-248-1946.
Visit our Web site at www.asq.org/quality-press.

 Printed on acid-free paper

Quality Press
600 N. Plankinton Ave.
Milwaukee, WI 53203-2914
E-mail: authors@asq.org

ASQ   The Global Voice of Quality™

Dedication

To my wife Alanna, whose love and encouragement makes this book possible.

Contents

List of Figures

Prologue

I, unfortunately, had to visit a cardiologist recently because of a poor stress test result. This, I am sure, is not unusual for people my age who are in the back half of the sixth decade. The doctor was faced with giving me the news that I needed an additional catheterization "procedure," as Billy Crystal, the comedian, would refer to it.

It is a fairly common procedure involving the insertion of a probe into the arteries of the heart, monitoring it on a live x-ray camera, checking out the amount of blockage, and then deciding whether remedial action such as angioplasty or stents or something more or less serious is required.

In explaining how straightforward this process is, the doctor explained that the risk of death was only 1 in 200, or 0.5 percent, so "how risky could it be." He seemed comfortable with that fact. I was terrified! I was scared not just because I am a cowardly male, but any manufacturer in the United States making ANYTHING, never mind a life-and-death product, with a 0.5 percent death rate would be out of business.

We worry about flying having a failure rate of less than one in a million. Yet, we are supposed to be OK with a death rate of 1 in 200 for a routine surgical "procedure"? Worse than that, he told me that he has done thousands of these (maybe an exaggeration) without a fatality. So, what the heck am I am supposed to take from that? As an old manufacturing guy, I suspected he was due some deaths to make the average work. Therefore, my fear!

However, I am obviously still here. Fortunately, the medical community has demonstrated a relentless pursuit of perfection. So, the surgical procedure was a success and I am one of the many medical miracles walking around today that a generation ago would not have been. The medical community has shown a tremendous capacity for making successful change.

As in the medical community, one of the greatest lessons learned about manufacturing products in the 20th century, which will continue to be true in the future, is the value of establishing an environment and mentality of continuous improvement toward the unachievable goal of perfection.

To achieve improvement, we need to change what we are doing. The old saying about insanity is true: If you keep doing what you are doing the way you are doing it, you will undoubtedly achieve the same result.

But making change is a pain!

As a small personal example, I once asked a group I was teaching to do something for me. "When you dress tomorrow," I said, "consciously change the sequence of putting on your socks and let's discuss how it felt tomorrow." The predominant feeling the next day was one of annoyance. People had to think about it, to do something different and for no great reason other than I had asked them to do it. I agreed with them that even small changes can be annoying.

I lived and worked in large companies for 35 years and have been asked many, many times to change what I was doing without any good reason, that I was aware of, so I didn't like it. So here is the lesson I learned and applied to a major corporate change: Spend time, a lot of time, understanding who is being asked to make a change. Who is affected by the change? Prepare a rationale for what they are being asked to do and explain why. Then figure out how the company can reward each of those groups of people for their successful participation. When making a decision about rewards and recognition, whether it is personal recognition, money, promotion, exposure to senior executive leadership, identification as role models, or any other form of reward, decide what it will be and do it. This means the traditional tee shirts, ball caps and belt buckles just won't cut it. Make the reward meaningful and reinforcing of the change you are making.

Then launch the program with all the fanfare of a product launch only focused internally.

Guess what...it works!

In this book, George Strodtbeck discusses in more detail the lessons he learned about making change than I have here. Some of these lessons we learned while we worked together at Cummins, Inc. It is my hope that the lessons he shares are helpful in making your own change plans successful.

FRANK J. MCDONALD
VICE PRESIDENT OF QUALITY (RETIRED)
CUMMINS, INC.

Acknowledgements

I have many people to thank for the support given to me through the years that made this book possible.

Frank McDonald, who authored the Prologue, is the best business guy I have ever known. Working with Frank for seven years at Cummins allowed me to learn from him and to try new things. Much of what I learned while working for Frank is reflected throughout the book.

Tim Solso and Joe Loughrey were the key leaders at Cummins who made it possible for Six Sigma to flourish and change the way people all over the company thought and worked.

Regina Clark gave me encouragement to continue writing when I wasn't sure if I had anything worthwhile to say. Her initial review and feedback were a great encouragement to me.

Jill Ronsley was my initial editor and provided great advice on how to tighten up my initial manuscript so that it reflected what I was thinking.

Professor Mohan Tatikonda reviewed and provided feedback during the book's final stages. He also invited me to participate in a Master's level course using the manuscript as part of his class. The student feedback from the class was very valuable to me in the final editing.

West Point and the disciplined education that it provided were critical to my understanding of leadership and how to work with people to accomplish great things.

There are so many others with whom I have worked through the years who have influenced my thinking and helped me to develop the ideas here. To all of them I owe a debt of gratitude for their teaching and cooperation during my working career.

1

An Introduction to Organization Change

THE AUDIENCE

This book is written for the leader or management team of any complex organization attempting to lead an organization-wide change. Successfully leading change has never been easy. Many realities of life in the 21st century have combined to intensify the challenge. I wrote this book to capture lessons learned over a 43-year working career and to share them in the hope that it will help others lead change successfully and avoid at least some of the pitfalls that come with it.

Many variables influence successful change. Organizations of all sizes today can include people around the globe who speak different languages and work both in offices or from home. Their customers, suppliers, and partners may be similarly multiple and highly distributed. Many employees speak English as a second language or not at all. In complex organizations, the impacts are magnified. A large organization can have 50 or more locations, an employee base of thousands of people, serving customers in in many different countries, with a multi-lingual, multi-segmented marketplace. Likewise, small organizations grapple with increasing complexity. An organization with as few as a dozen employees at only one site can be complex due to different areas of expertise for each employee and variation in customers, suppliers, and partners. In all organization types, many, if not most, of the people who work there have little connection to those who originally started it. These are just a few of the variables impacting our ability to make changes successfully.

Often these organizations are companies, but the ideas laid out in this book can also be applied outside of the business world.

The principles and questions in this book also benefit leaders making changes in the small organization or those who desire to transform their small organization into a large one. This book is intended to serve as a leaders' guide of things to think about and how to plan for successful change.

LEADERS AS BUILDERS

This is a book primarily for leaders who are builders. A simple example will illustrate what I mean by "builder." In America, prior to the 1500s, it is said the trees in the eastern half of the continent were so dense that a squirrel could travel across the treetops from the Mississippi River to the Atlantic Ocean and never touch the ground. Pioneers and explorers began moving into these areas to explore, trap, hunt and, often, to get away from civilized society. Builders followed the pioneers. The builders were the farmers, ranchers, merchants, and others who built the infrastructure that over two-plus centuries later became the United States of today.

Pioneers were not the right people to clear and farm the land. They were generally not interested in creating livable towns and cities. It takes people who are interested in staying in one place to build the infrastructure necessary for the maintenance of society. A comparison in a healthy, modern organization is the critical role played by those with an entrepreneurial spirit. They are like the pioneers stretching the organization to pursue new products, new regions, and new customers. This activity keeps the organization growing. Building and running the plants, creating and sustaining the organizational culture, and developing secure jobs for people tends to belong to those who build the infrastructure. A healthy organization needs both pioneers and builders.

The builders in an organization are those who tend not to want to move a lot. They are content where they are and like to see things through. Builders are willing to grow in a job or profession and hope to rise into senior executive leadership positions within a specific skill or functional area. They are motivated to learn more about what they do and continuously improving. They tend to be willing to spend whatever time it takes to do what needs to be done. The builders tend to put as much emphasis on "how" the work is done as on the results.

My intent for the organizational pioneers is that they use this book to understand that leading, managing, and changing an organization takes perseverance and time. A person needs to learn how the organization responds, make course corrections, and struggle with the complex issues that come with changing what people do every day. Therefore, the work described in this book can consume five to ten years or more, especially in the larger organization. This means that the pioneers and the builders have to work together and see the value in the role that each plays.

These descriptions are intentionally simplistic. I'm not writing a psychology book. And, to reiterate, both pioneers and builders are valuable and necessary to the organization. However, the pioneers tend not to be the right people to lead organization-wide change. They need to be involved. A pioneer might even be a sponsor, but they tend to be the wrong people to be the direct leaders, that is, the hands on executers of change, because it simply takes too much time.

I am not advocating a "trust me, this just takes time" approach. There is no point in doing any of this if results don't begin showing real improvement. For a company, this means more profit. For non-profit organizations, it translates, for example, to more people served. I am advocating a balance between short- and long-term actions; balance that is planned and includes selecting the right people to drive a change successfully.

Many books have been written about management and leadership as well as the dos and must-dos of leading an organization. Some of them are good; some are not so good. In my experience, few books discuss what it takes to make changes in today's complex organizations. It is a daunting task and there aren't a lot of people with experience doing it who have taken the time to write down what they have learned.

What also makes it difficult is that consultants who write, sell, and then move on tend to write much of the literature on the subject. They often don't engage long enough to see the outcome of their advice over time. The time required to see the impact of systemic changes made in complex organizations takes more time than the consultant can or is willing to give. In most cases, it's impossible to thoroughly communicate a multi-year plan during the consulting intervention, let alone see the impacts and make adjustments to the plan. Consultants have their place, and I will discuss that later, but delivering the desired change and results is not one of them. Change requires commitment to the organization and its people and a clear vision of a better future. Only the organization's leadership has this capability.

So, the need exists to draw lessons from a successful long-term change made by leaders having a personal and financial stake in the organization's success who saw it all the way through. This is the gap that I am attempting to help fill with this book.

WHY IS THIS BOOK DIFFERENT?

This book is different because it captures the lessons I have learned during more than 43 years of experience working in complex, large-scale organizations, 14 years between West Point and the United States Army, and more than 29 years in two large, very different American companies.

My best experience in leading change happened while working for Cummins, Inc., a large, global company that designs, manufactures, sells, and services diesel and natural gas power equipment and components. During the two decades I worked there, I spent 16 years implementing Six Sigma, more than 10 years developing and deploying a business operating system, as well as involvement in other efforts.

In the Army, I learned about discipline, leadership, communication and the value of believing in something larger than oneself. In the business world, I have learned many things about how the change process does and doesn't work.

There was no book that could tell us how to make change in my organizations. There was no advisor that could be called upon. We could benchmark and study and ask the advice of consultants. And we did. However, when it came to execution and seeing the change through, we were on our own and, mostly, we just made it up as we went along. I have been a part of more failures than successes. It is the failures that led to the successes and gave me the desire to write it all down.

This book is built on principles and concepts that developed over time and guided that journey. It is not a cookbook or a plug-and-play template. Rather it is a set of guidelines, things to think about, and critical elements to consider when leading change. Overall, I want the reader to see a framework for decision making and action that improves the chances of success.

SIX SIGMA AS AN EXAMPLE OF HOW TO MAKE CHANGE

The deployment of Six Sigma at Cummins, Inc. is one of the most successful change efforts that I have participated and led. Therefore, throughout the book I use Six Sigma as a specific example to illustrate lessons learned that could be extended to other large-scale changes.

However, I am also quite aware that Six Sigma can be used as one of the best examples of how change efforts fail, as was described in an article about implementing Six Sigma initiatives in the July 11, 2006 issue of *Fortune Magazine.*[i] Failure tends to be the result when Six Sigma is seen too narrowly and not allowed to grow and mature. When deployed correctly over time, Six Sigma focuses on problems and improvements that have a measureable impact on customers and business results. In its pure form, Six Sigma uses statistical analysis of data and cross-functional teams of subject matter experts to identify the root cause or causes of problems so that they can be quickly solved. My discussion will use examples of the deployment of Six Sigma to describe how to make change successfully.

My experience is that Six Sigma, or any change, will be as small or as expansive as it's allowed to be. The major ingredient for culture change is leadership that is committed to the change and willing to devote the time to learn how to best apply and grow it in one's organization. In the Six Sigma example, this basic requirement was a foundation of the successful deployment at Cummins that built a new culture of continuous improvement. However, this potential is lost on those who think implementing a Six Sigma initiative is all about training, statistics, belts, and project savings, instead of using it to create something new.

The culture of an organization includes the language used to communicate. Think of health care or automobile repair or a soccer team. The people involved have a language that is unique to their organization and what they do. Using Six Sigma as an example shows how a change pursued over time can result in the adoption of a common language for creating and sustaining change and is not limited to tools, statistics, and training. The nuances of this are lost on those who don't give Six Sigma the time necessary to understand it. This is true of any broad-based change that an organization tries to make. So, although this is not a book about Six Sigma, I will use examples from this process because successfully creating a Six Sigma culture or mindset contains elements that are the same as the elements found in any major change effort. Using lessons learned from Six Sigma and other change implementations, I will devote most of the book to discussing things that leaders can do that both lead to success and help avoid the barriers that can derail a change effort.

2

The Importance of the Goal

THE AIRCRAFT CARRIER

Running a complex organization is not a mystery—examples abound. My favorite is the aircraft carrier. A United States Navy aircraft carrier (Figure 2.1) is the most complex machine ever created by man. It's really a small city floating on the ocean. It is approximately 300 meters long by 100 meters wide and is designed for a service life of 50 years. It is run by two nuclear reactors that can keep the ship at sea continuously for 20 years without refueling and carries 90 aircraft. It also houses 6,000 people and meets all of their food, clothing, sleeping, working, and general living needs. It is an amazing feat of

Figure 2.1 The aircraft carrier USS Nimitz at sea.

https://commons.wikimedia.org/wiki/File:USS_Nimitz_(CVN-68).jpg

design, engineering, and construction. But there is something even more amazing—the aircraft carrier is run largely by young men and women in their early to mid-twenties.

An aircraft carrier stays afloat and conducts its mission at sea through a combination of discipline, individual and collective skills, communication, and clarity of purpose or the goal. The people are not generally smarter or more capable than those in other organizational groups. There is, however, a priority placed on training, as well as the measurement of individual skills and capability that is directly connected to the accomplishment of the goal that I find generally lacking in many organizations outside the military.

An example of this lack of connection to the organizational goal happened during my transition from the Army in 1986 to my first job in a private company. I had not been a civilian since the age of 18 and had never worked in the corporate world. The closest I had come to working in business was working for a summer in the local root beer stand pouring soft drinks and handing out picklewiches (a "picklewich" is exactly what it sounds like: a bunch of pickles on a warm bun). Therefore, I was a complete novice at everything. Nevertheless, on the day I arrived for my new job, my boss met me at the airport and drove me to the garage in the building where I was going to be the maintenance supervisor. He walked me into the building, waved his arm in a broad arc and said, "Well, here's where you're going to work. I'll see you in three months." Then he walked out of the building and flew back to his office in another state. Imagine running an aircraft carrier this way. It would sink!

The modern organization with its need to follow ever-expanding rules, laws and regulations, continuous communications requirements, constantly changing customer and employee demands, and a 24/7 world lives at a level of dynamism that can seem every bit as complex as that of an aircraft carrier. If an aircraft carrier can be successfully run and maintained by young sailors, shouldn't it be easier to run the modern complex organization by a collection of MBAs, PhDs and others who have basically done the same thing their entire adult lives? Clear goals that are well communicated, resourced, and supported will drive what people in the organization do. This is a critical element of successful organizational change.

THE GOAL—DEFINING THE "WHY"

Clearly defining why the organization exists gives people who work in it a clear understanding of where they are going, a reason for staying, and a knowledge of the focus of improvement.

Is your goal to be the best in the world in your chosen industry? Is the goal to be an example of philanthropic achievements for others to follow?

Random Action   Aligned and Synchronized

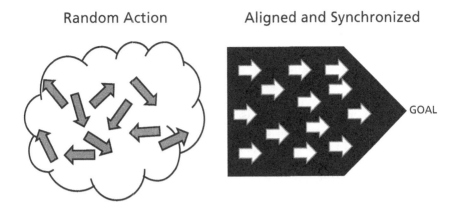

GOAL

Figure 2.2 Moving from random action to aligned and synchronized action.

Does the organization intend to establish a basis of societal advancement in a third world region? Is the goal steady, sustained growth over the long term? Is the goal rapid growth with an eye toward appreciation, mergers, and acquisitions?

Not every person in the company is looking to become a millionaire or a captain of industry. Many, if not most, simply desire to have a good life. They want to raise their families, put a decent roof over their heads, have nice things, and to have a good standard of living. Further, in the global organization, the definition of "good standard of living" is quite variable, an issue not always well understood by the policy makers in the home office. A goal that creates a sense of pride in the people of the organization gives the organization great power and purpose that goes beyond the simple measures of profit and loss. This power and purpose comes from all the people in the organization as they align together to achieve a common objective. The alignment of organization resources (people, time, and money) is a leadership challenge that well-stated goals can help to overcome.

The basic idea of alignment is that the organization's ultimate success is dependent on its ability to get its resources working together rather than relying on best efforts or random actions that may or may not have a positive impact on the goals of the organization (Figure 2.2). Relying on random actions is analogous to the old adage that if you put an infinite number of monkeys in a room together with an infinite number of typewriters, all of Shakespeare's sonnets would eventually be written. Most organizations don't have infinite resources or time! And, the old adage probably isn't right anyway.

One example is the aircraft carrier. Another example of alignment can be seen in the United States Army. One of the unique aspects of the military is its ability to establish alignment through common goals and objectives and then to hold people accountable for goal accomplishment. This organizational alignment in the United States Army (and the other military branches as well) begins at the swearing-in stage where the members commit to support and defend the Constitution of the United States of America. All activity is connected to and aligned with this pledge. It is significant that the most effective fighting force in human history has grown from a fealty to a clear higher purpose.

However, the military is enabled by a strong command and control structure that is difficult, if not impossible, to replicate outside of the military environment. Most people don't like working under such a strict command structure and will choose to leave for less strict cultures. But the command structure is not what is important; the idea of alignment is what's important. The challenge for an organization's leadership is to make the goal and purpose meaningful to diverse people who can choose where to work.

What connects the activity of manufacturing sites, sales organizations, design engineers, customer support, finance, and the various other functions of an organization together? Is it the connection to profit in the case of a business? Is the connection doing good things in the case of a non-profit? Lacking direction derived from a common goal, people simply end up working independently in the hopes of pleasing their bosses because the boss has power over their paycheck, promotions, the kind of work they get to do, and whether they are allowed to stay in the organization.

If money is the organization's primary goal, each individual will tend to do whatever maximizes his or her own personal income. This will be encouraged by senior executive leadership in the belief that maximizing individual profit will result in maximizing business profits as well.

The reality is that people often work at cross-purposes and utilize organizational resources that actually work against success. For example, bonus plans are often set up to reward local objectives. Achievement of local objectives may work against interdependencies between organizations. Lack of working together ultimately damages overall organizational performance. In another example, marketing and sales departments often have volume or revenue targets as the prime directive without a clear understanding of or responsibility for the costs of running the organization that affect the profit margins required to sustain and grow the business. At the same time, another part of the organization may be focused on the high-profit-margin business selling fewer, more highly profitable products.

I have observed this exact situation play out. The senior executive leadership at a local business was rewarded by corporate for selling package A. This meant local senior executive leadership wanted to sell lots of package A. The junior management was rewarded for total volume sold. This meant they wanted to move lots of package B because that's what consumers tended to want most. Senior executive leadership was continually frustrated by the failure of junior management to hit its package A targets, but never struggling to meet targets for package B. By the way, both groups were in the same building separated only by the floor between them. They failed to see how competing objectives were having a negative impact on the organization.

There was no maliciousness here. People were just trying to do the best they could to do with what they thought was being asked of them. In this simple (real) example, it is easy to see how a clearly-communicated, common goal reinforced by compatible incentives would have created an alignment of resources to apply the organization's power to achieve a desired result. Of course, the challenge is often not this simple and direct.

Given the potential consequences of misalignment, an important management task is to organize to achieve specific goals and objectives. Two tools, the future state and the Goal Tree, help to accomplish this.

I have become increasingly convinced that a well-crafted future state description is necessary for any organization to be successful. It documents, in detail, the behaviors and actions that will be seen in the future if improvements are successful. I have often been a participant in a conversation that ends, "I don't exactly know what it is, but I'll know it when I see it." The future state helps paint the picture of what it will look like and establishes a baseline for communication and planning, taking the guesswork out of what the future might look like. It gives leadership something concrete to develop, agree to, and own. It also creates traceability that lives through assignment and role changes, helping to keep the organization moving forward. If the desired changes aren't documented, how will leadership ever know when they get there? The answer is, they won't and therefore, it becomes easy to jump from initiative to initiative because there is no defined end state that is agreed upon and pursued.

The future state is used to identify the long-term goals and objectives that the organization will pursue. It is also reviewed on an annual basis and it generates and validates changes over time. The review keeps the future state consistent with changing conditions and keeps it grounded in reality. It is broadly communicated and discussed, and is the starting point for improvement planning.

Communicating this view of the future to an organization's employees is an important step to ensure that employees understand and buy into the organization's future direction.

The Goal Tree (Figure 2.3) highlights short- to medium-term improvement initiatives and projects that are necessary to achieve future goals.

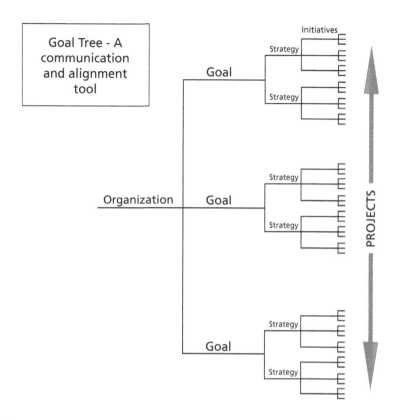

Figure 2.3 The Goal Tree.

The Goal Tree is an alignment and communication tool that ensures that everyone in the organization can see how their work contributes to the broader established goals and objectives.

A difficult challenge for most organizations is sticking with any change long enough to see the impact of that change on results. An organization's leadership may be tempted to declare victory based on anecdotal, short-term results, but real change takes time. It is arduous, often repetitive work and can become boring during the middle phases of the change.

The implementation of a new idea always starts with a lot of enthusiasm, but as time moves along, enthusiasm flags. This is the dark night of the innovator (Figure 2.4).[ii] It happens in virtually all change efforts. The more complex the organization, the more impactful the "Dark Night" is because of the increased time it takes for change to occur. It is imperative that leadership perseveres or changes will fail to achieve their hoped for result.

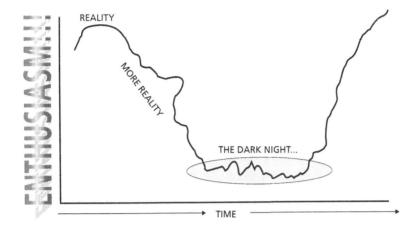

Figure 2.4 The Dark Night of the innovator.

WHAT IT TAKES

The best example of this perseverance is Cummins CEO Tim Solso's personal effort from 1999 to 2011 during the company's adoption of Six Sigma. As the tactical leader of the effort, I was privileged to have a front row seat.

Cummins' Six Sigma journey started when Tim was selected as Cummins CEO in 1998. He had been with the company for 30 years and was committed to improving the company's performance. He started by discussing the role with other CEOs. During this time, he learned about Six Sigma from two CEOs; one was the CEO of a Cummins' customer and another was CEO of a supplier to Cummins. Tim decided to learn more about this new idea.

At the time, General Electric was receiving a lot of publicity about its use of Six Sigma to improve business results. Tim scheduled a visit with a vice president of one of GE's businesses. The business that Tim visited was a commodity electrical components business, and therefore, profitability tended to be stable without much room for growth. Tim took Frank McDonald to the meeting. Frank was selected to lead Quality and the Six Sigma implementation because his years of experience in operations, which gave him credibility with the operations people in the company. Tim asked the GE VP if Six Sigma was real or just a PR gambit on the part of the GE CEO. The GE VP told them that when Six Sigma first started, the other GE leaders weren't convinced and were reluctant to spend much time on it. However, some of the businesses tried it and began showing results. Slowly the other GE businesses got on board. He told them that the results had been stunning. This commodity business had grown profitability by 6 percent over five years and Six Sigma was the cause. This was all Tim needed to hear.

On returning to the company, Tim began to lead what would become one of the most successful change efforts in company history.

To kick-start this change effort, a consultant was selected based on the quality of the individual consultants who would lead our account. A contract was written licensing the consulting company's training material and committing them to a transfer of their knowledge to Cummins over two years to make us self-sufficient and then leaving on December 31, 2001. This was a critical element of Cummins' Six Sigma transformation as it forced people in the company to learn and understand what Six Sigma was really all about. I will discuss more about the consulting approach in a later chapter.

Tim also required the senior executive leadership to attend two days of overview training. He established a requirement that the first group of Black Belts (full-time project leaders) would be among the company's best employees and handpicked based on their past performance.

In January 2000 Cummins launched its first three training classes. These classes were comprised of 68 Black Belts from around the world and represented all company departments and businesses from HR and finance to engineering and manufacturing.

Even more important to Six Sigma's success at Cummins was what Tim did following the launch of the effort. In April 2000, he attended the first Green Belt training launch (Green Belts work on projects as part of their normal work) and completed a project to improve Cummins' approach to its bonus program. At the same time, he scheduled to meet monthly for one to two hours with a Master Black Belt (the technical experts and trainers) to learn the processes and tools of Six Sigma. Tim also scheduled time with Belts and project Sponsors to review projects in private in order to increase his understanding of how Six Sigma worked. In June 2001, Tim and his executive leadership team attended a four-day refresher course focused on the tools used in Six Sigma and on four successful projects showing Six Sigma's potential. Following this review, Six Sigma became part of Tim's monthly leadership team's agenda. The monthly Six Sigma review would begin with a measures review followed by two presentations of recently completed projects. This continued every month for eight years. Additionally, during visits to Cummins facilities around the world, Tim would schedule time with Belts to discuss Six Sigma with them and find out if the process was truly working. The example Tim set showed how important Six Sigma was to the success of the company and what he expected from other leaders.

Cummins was a good company, but not a great one. Tim wanted it to be great. Six Sigma became a key element for achieving his vision for the future. Without Tim's direct involvement and direction, the attempt to use Six Sigma would probably have ended up just like many other

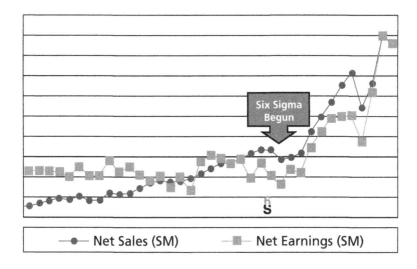

Figure 2.5 The effect of Six Sigma on net revenue and net earnings.

improvement efforts that had been tried before—unrealized potential. As of the end of 2014, the company's 21,000 Belts had completed over 45,000 projects resulting in savings of over five billion dollars. The effect of Six Sigma is best seen in the accompanying chart (Figure 2.5) taken from public information available from company annual reports. The profitability of Cummins dramatically changed during this period. None of it would have been possible if the Cummins CEO, Tim Solso, hadn't spent 11 years focused on this massive, company-wide change effort.

> *The realization: Nobody is standing behind you in the mirror...it is up to you to do it.*

All organization leaders must eventually realize that they are in this alone. There is no book, consultant, benchmark, or board of directors that can tell you how to make change in your organization. Nobody is standing behind you in the mirror—there is only you.

So what are you going to do? How are you going to lead the people who depend on your decisions? This book won't tell you how to run your unique organization, but it will give you ideas to consider when making change and offer tools that might aid the process of organizing for success. How these tools are used depends on the unique culture and purpose of each individual organization.

3

Leadership: The Indispensable Ingredient

The indispensable ingredient in broad change efforts is leadership. I have observed through my years in the military and in business that the organization reflects the leader. This observation was most acute in the Army where leadership changes were frequent. A well-ordered, by-the-book, disciplined battalion would change into a sloppy, mistake-prone, disorderly band of misfits within a few short weeks or months following a change of command if a new leader's approaches to unit discipline were significantly different from the previous leader's. Priorities change, standards relax, discipline slides, and new people are poorly integrated into the unit. All of this and more happen based on the personality, likes, and dislikes of the new commander. It is no different in non-military organizations. The leader sets the tone. The leader decides what is important and how directive, collaborative, or laissez-faire to be.

A simple breakdown of the levels of leadership and their different roles is reflected in Figure 3.1 and includes:

- Senior executive – Sets vision and direction, communicates with the Board of Directors, determines priorities, allocates resources.

- Junior executive – Develops supporting plans, coordinates resources, monitors use of resources.

- Senior management – Develops local support plans, assigns resources, distributes the resources.

- Junior management – Executes plans and uses resources.

For purposes of this book, discussions of leadership will be in the context of these levels with primary focus on the role of Senior Executive leadership.

Senior executives are human beings, and fallible, just like everyone else. But, sometimes leaders forget how important they are to the health and success of the organization. They have risen to an important position through the combination of hard work, a pattern of success, timing, luck, and sometimes knowing the right people.

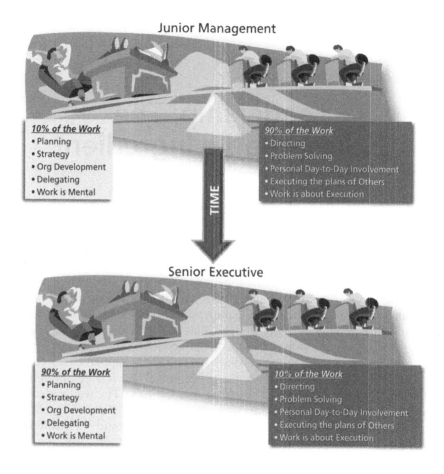

Figure 3.1 Levels of leadership and their roles.

So, average leaders forget. They forget that people look to them for guidance. They forget that some people will do anything to please them. And they forget that some people in the organization may view them as infallible.

It may be that leaders haven't actually forgotten all of this; they may have never really known or considered this reality. Leadership is all about people. Things are managed; people are led. It is people who bring about change. What leadership does or doesn't do determines whether or not a change is going to succeed. Leadership is the indispensable ingredient. Therefore, the process for developing and selecting leaders must be planned and deployed as a critical activity of the organization.

MANAGEMENT CAPITAL

Large-scale change develops and matures over time. This requires a continuity of leadership action providing a stable direction that comes from consistent goals and objectives reinforced by how management capital is spent.

During a strategy and leadership conference in the 1990s, I first heard the concept of management capital. The organization's leadership demonstrates what is valued by how it spends its time, money, personal energy, and enthusiasm. This is analogous to the everyday activities that one sees in any store. A customer shows the storeowner what items are valuable by taking time to go to the store, walk the aisles, pick an item, hand the cashier money in trade for the item, and leave the store with it. This is how consumers demonstrate what they value.

Similarly, leadership demonstrates what it values by how it spends its personal energy and enthusiasm, time, and resources. What the leader values can be seen in daily appointments, budgets, and personal excitement. If any of the elements of management capital are missing, the people in the organization know the activity is not that important. The result is minimal effort. The trappings of support for the change may be there, but the real work that people do is directed towards other things that are "really important." Spending management capital is hard work for leadership because, similar to personal spending, the capital that a manager has to spend is finite. There are only so many hours in the day, only so much money to be spent on the myriad competing priorities, and only a limited amount of personal energy and enthusiasm to devote to any single initiative.

Management capital is allocated based on priorities. Leaders cannot spend more capital than they have available. Overspending works against the success of both the change effort and other priorities. Therefore, how the leader decides to spend their management capital will have a direct impact on what the people of the organization do. They will watch what leadership does and doesn't do. People tend to work and focus where management is seen spending its scarce capital. The organization's employees look at the following:

- The areas where the leader is spending time planning, helping, and reviewing the work.

- The areas where the leader is allocating funds, budgeting for work to be done, and monitoring how effectively the money is being spent. Of equal importance, employees will notice the areas where money is being taken away for the funding of other priorities.

- The areas where the leader is enthusiastically engaged and excited about the work. What the leader is communicating about via e-mail, blogs, quarterly newsletters, annual meetings, etc.

The spending of management capital and its impact on a planned change reinforces the notion that leadership is the indispensable ingredient.

THREE LEADERSHIP IMPEDIMENTS TO SUCCESSFUL CHANGE

Leadership, the indispensable ingredient, fundamentally influences success and failure. Three leadership phenomena—Fast Trackers, the Peter Principle, and the Big Boom—commonly occur in all sorts of organizations. It is helpful to be aware of them and correct for them if necessary. Do any of these occur in your organization?

1. The Leadership Fast Track

A bias toward fast tracking future senior executive leaders can act as an impediment to organization-wide change. In some organizations, there is a perception that only fast-tracking managers are valued. In many modern organizations, it is expected that high-potential employees be on a fast track to the executive suite. The fast track means that the employee moves higher in the organization, at a minimum, every two to three years. These moves are accompanied by promotions and increased responsibility. Often, these fast-trackers are sponsored and mentored by an existing executive who sees "something special" in the person with high potential.

The habit of rapid moves and jumping from one thing to another is engrained early in the fast-tracker's career. In fact, when things aren't happening fast, when moves aren't happening every 18 months to two years, it can feel like failure.

So an organizational norm of "things happen fast here" is established. When they don't happen fast, it's an indication that something is wrong. There are both positives and negatives of this approach but the negative impact on large-scale change can be dramatic.

Often, this process is influenced by the perception that failure of the fast-tracker reflects poorly on the sponsor. The roots of this perception lie in the assumption that a failed fast-tracker is failure by the sponsor to deliver on one of his/her key responsibilities: developing the organization's future leaders. Therefore, because of this factor, once on the fast track it becomes difficult, sometimes impossible, to fall off because there is so much at stake for so many.

To be clear, this approach doesn't always fail. It has, in fact, produced some great leaders. Dwight Eisenhower is one of my favorite examples of a successful fast-tracker. The story of his rise to the presidency of the United States is both amazing and interesting with many facets to the story. He was successful, and once on the fast track, it took him to the top. So fast-tracking can work. But as a successful strategy for large-scale change, it brings with it the possibility of real and critical failure.

Change in complex organizations requires time and effort, accompanied by patience and repetition. This is not the strong suit of the fast-tracker. It is not encouraged or even seen as a positive characteristic. Seeing real, measurable changes in results and culture generally doesn't happen in two or three years.

If the people who are leading and sponsoring the change are ingrained with fast-tracker habits, they begin getting antsy after 18 months and bored after 24. They are ready to move on to the next promotion or job challenge and are encouraged to do so. Worse, feelings of failure and of being passed over begin to creep in as time moves beyond the two-year mark. This can create panic in the fast-tracker, resulting in strenuous efforts to prove themselves worthy of being on the fast track, further eroding any possible success of a large-scale change effort because there is more focus on personal career ambitions than on the change activities.

Finally, if sufficiently frustrated, the fast-tracker will start looking for greener pastures in another company, beginning the cycle all over again with the next high-potential candidate.

So, in the fast-track leadership environment, the change is handed off to somebody else. Priorities are redefined or modified. Ownership of the change is disrupted. It doesn't take long for the change effort to atrophy. Organizational rigor mortis sets in and the change effort disappears from the organization's priorities.

A personal example of this phenomenon comes in the late 1980s in my first job after the military when I was working as a fleet manager. One of my goals was to improve the length of time that each of the delivery trucks was in service. Having established a 20-year useful-life plan to extend the life of the franchise's vehicles, I was anxious to show it to the senior VP who was the leader in that business. He had just arrived a few weeks earlier and this was one of my first meetings with him. I set up the time and put the relevant charts and graphs together in preparation for our meeting.

When the appointed time came, I launched into my analysis: what we would have to do, how much money this would save, and so on. About midway through the discussion, the VP stopped me. What he said next shocked me at the time, but in retrospect, helped to partly explain why it is so hard to make changes in complex organizations. He told me he had never held a job in the company longer than 24 months. This job was another step on his path to senior executive leadership and he wouldn't be here beyond the required 18 to 24 months. He thought what I was doing was important and necessary, but he just didn't care, because he wouldn't be around long enough for my plans to make any difference in how he ran the franchise.

Now, this is just one example and it comes from personal experience. One data point does not make a trend, but ask yourself, is it possible that this type of behavior is playing itself out in your organization because of the expectations that have been created as a result of the way people are promoted and move? Will a five- to ten-year change effort succeed in your organization given the constant churn that exists in the leadership ranks? These questions are worth answering to assess whether your organization's leadership development approach is driving the behavior that is necessary for successful continuous improvement.

2. The Peter Principle

Another failure in making changes for organizational success is the *Peter Principle*. The Peter Principle states: "in a hierarchy every employee tends to rise to his level of incompetence."

One sees it happening over and over again as an organization's leadership struggles to keep the leadership pipeline filled. The problem is that most employee management systems are inadequate for this purpose. For example, the performance management systems and the people who use them tend to focus on what a person has accomplished in their assessment period. These systems are quite adequate in describing what has happened in the past, but are much less useful when it comes to assessing a person's competence to handle the responsibilities that come with the next and future levels. Assessing what a person has done is like driving while looking in the rear view mirror. Assessing the potential of someone to be a future leader by looking at what one has done in the past is to answer all the wrong questions. A facet of why this is so difficult is Figure 3.1 shown earlier. The responsibilities of the junior leader tend to be primarily action-oriented with some minor future-oriented thinking regarding strategy, analysis and planning. The higher one climbs the organizational leadership ladder, the more the responsibilities shift from action to thinking and planning. But, because the system and the people running it are mostly concerned with what a person has accomplished, an objective analysis of whether the person is capable of functioning in the executive suite and leading large-scale organizational change is marginally effective at best. Performance management systems seek, generally, to assess the following:

- How well did this person complete their assigned work plan?
- How did this person perform against assigned measures?
- What performance gaps exist? What actions need to be taken to close these gaps?

The other problem with current performance systems is that people who have generally never served in senior levels of the organization and therefore don't understand the requirements from a personal viewpoint are using the systems to evaluate an individual's potential for a higher position. Furthermore, the people who have served in the higher roles and understand what it takes to lead are typically far removed from the people in the junior ranks and can't possibly know them well enough to assess their potential. Advancement, then, is based on what people have done, not on what they have the potential to do. And so, people get promoted beyond their true capability, bringing to life the Peter Principle. This approach is not a complete failure, as some competent people do rise. However, it tends to be a trial and error process, and the failures are many and costly both in terms of mistakes made and development money spent.

Some of the best examples of the Peter Principle that I have seen happen in areas of strong functional expertise. A person proves to be great in their functional role. This person rises through the ranks of the function through personal contributions, but rarely has true responsibility for leading other people. The fact that the person doesn't really know how to lead people remains hidden until the first manager or executive leadership role. The person struggles and is seen as a failure, but the real failure is that the system was incapable of correctly assessing that this person's value to the organization is as an individual contributor not as a leader. The effect of this organizational failure is that a bright, capable person has had his or her confidence shaken, several people have been poorly led and now question the quality of his or her performance, and organizational performance has been diminished. Effective change stands no chance of success in this type of leadership environment.

3. The Big Boom

Another characteristic of failed change that can be seen in a complex organization is the Big Boom phenomenon. Leadership that has a fascination for the next great thing characterizes the Big Boom. There is a general perception that launching a new program is all that is required. The dominant belief is that once people realize the overwhelming logic and importance of the launched program, they will carry it off without the need for senior executive leadership oversight.

The Big Boom phenomenon looks like this: Imagine a giant cannon hanging over the ocean. The cannon represents the newest, organization-saving program. Gathered around the cannon is senior executive leadership. The cannon roars to life with fire, smoke, and a giant BOOM! The boom is the launch of the new program. With a lot of fanfare, senior executive leadership has just launched the next great program. They are all excited and cheer the cannon ball on its way as it splashes into the ocean (the organization).

After the boom and splash, what happens? The ocean quickly absorbs the cannon ball's energy. The cannon ball slowly drifts to the bottom of the ocean where it sits, covered with silt as time and leadership moves on. Meanwhile, leadership expects the boom and cannon ball to have made a difference in the organization. They may come back to check on the status from time to time, but the momentum of the initiative has long since been lost. Leadership then starts looking for the next BIG BOOM.

If you look on the bookshelves of the leaders of any complex organization, you are apt to find, scattered here and there, three-ring binders representing the various programs launched over the years. These binders often have a colorful, uniquely-designed logo and contain the notes taken during the training session. These binders are also typically covered with dust and haven't been opened since the original training. Copies of these dust-covered binders will also be found spread around the organization.

Successful implementation of any organizational change, be it large or small, is *always* difficult. And, importantly, deployment of organization-wide change is not only difficult but is simply impossible absent the indispensable ingredient—leadership.

4

Defining the Change

As the indispensable ingredient, an organization's leadership is responsible for several actions fundamental to successful change. The purpose of all actions is to ultimately change what people do in order to realize the potential benefits of the desired change. There are a number of key questions that leadership needs to answer to help the employees understand the need for change:

1. Where are we now?

2. Where are we going and what will be different when we get there? (This is the description of the organization's future state.)

3. What change are we making?

4. Why is this change important to leadership?

5. Why is this change important to customers?

6. Why is it important to employees?

7. How are we going to get there?

8. What are employees supposed to do?

9. What is leadership going to do to help employees?

10. What is the incentive for making or not making the expected changes?

What follows is a discussion of some of the actions leadership can take to answer these questions and lead a successful change effort in a complex organization.

WHERE ARE WE NOW?

The first step is to assess the current state of the organization. An assessment answers questions describing how the organization is doing relative to its goals and objectives. The Baldrige Criteria provides a solid framework for assessing an organization.

Answering the following questions can be instrumental to creating a current state:

1. What is the purpose of the organization?

2. How are things working today?

3. Is the organization successful? How do you know?

4. How is success measured?

5. In what areas is the organization less successful than desired?

6. Are the organization's customers happy with the products and services received? How do you know? What do your customers think of your competition?

7. Are the organization's people happy working here? How do you know?

8. What are the known performance gaps?

9. What needs to change to make the organization better?

The answers to these questions lead to a decision. The organization's leadership can decide to do something or decide not to do something in order to make the organization different in the future. Only the organization's leadership can make this decision. Assuming that the answer is to do something different (the other answer would cause me to stop right here), the following is a discussion of what to do:

Where are we going and what will be different when we get there? The answer is the creation of the future state. (How to create a future state is discussed in Chapter 7).

The future state is a valuable document for organizational change. People want to know where they are going and what is expected of them. The communication of expectations is difficult and time consuming. The future state is a structured approach to describing where the organization is headed and ultimately leads to a definition of everyone's role in making it happen.

The purpose of a future state is organizational alignment. The future state tends to be subjective. It illuminates the difference between how things are now and how they will be after the changes have occurred. A future state describes what people will be doing differently following the change effort. It is the mirror that the organization holds up to itself in order to see how close it is to where it wants to go.

Organizational alignment occurs as the future state is communicated. The goal of communicating the future state is to enroll people into supporting the need for the changes that are to be made. This is not a one-way process and is often iterative. Leadership drafts the future state and develops a communication and feedback plan. The communication plan lets people know where the organization is headed while the feedback plan improves and validates what becomes the word picture (a description in words of what the organization looks like) of the organization's future.

The details of the future state are enhanced and improved as new information becomes available through time, but the basic direction is set and provides context for all the change activity to follow. When the future state is finalized, it is expected that the entire leadership team agrees to support and be involved in the changes necessary to make the future state a reality.

For those leaders who show after a reasonable period of time ("reasonable period" must be clearly defined) that they are unwilling to actively engage in achieving the future state, it must be clear that this is not an option. These leaders must be invited to find other employment regardless of their current rank and position. In the book *Good to Great* by Jim Collins, this is called getting the right people on the bus. While these are difficult actions to take, the naysayers (and there will be some no matter how compelling the potential future state) will undermine any change effort, making it difficult to succeed in the long run.

WHAT CHANGE WE WILL MAKE?

What do I mean by *change*? Change means that the whole organization is following the new approach, using the new system, working to the new standards, and speaking with one voice. This kind of change is far-reaching, permanent, and structural.

For example, in a global organization gaining agreement and following a common standard as it applies to bribery is difficult. In most of the West, bribery is against the law; in other parts of the world giving somebody money to win an account isn't bribery at all, but simply the way business is done. Changing this behavior is complicated.

A way to begin the change process is to consider change efforts that had been undertaken previously. The answers can give you clues to the culture of your organization.

First, think about a successful change. Why was the change successful?

- Did the idea for change bubble up from the bottom or was it driven from the top?
- How was the need for change communicated?
- What role did leadership play in the successful change? Who was perceived as the leader of the change?
- How was success measured? How do you know the change was successful?
- How long was the change given to work?

Now, identify a change that was unsuccessful:

- Why did the change fail?
- What were the expectations for the change?
- How was the change communicated?
- Who led the change?
- What role did the organization's leadership play in the change? What did they really do?
- How much of the organization's time, money, and other resources were spent on the change? What was the return on investment (ROI)?
- Who took the fall for the failure of the change?

Use the responses to these questions in the development of the change plan.

THE BEGINNING—A GREAT IDEA

Typically change begins with a great idea. There are many great ideas out there. Some ideas come from the organization's leaders and employees, some from consultants, others come from academics, some come from government, and still others come from other companies. The leadership of an organization can hear about these great ideas from friends, books, conferences, customers, or suppliers. The leaders may even do some research to learn more about the idea and discuss the idea's feasibility. Generally, for the change to be successful, it is important that the change idea be connected to the organization's future state. Following are some discussions that leaders may have when contemplating change.

One of the first discussions looks at whether the change is even necessary. Things may be pretty good in the organization so people may wonder if they really need to make a change. Objections such as concern about the lack of resources to tackle both the change and taking care of our current customers may also be raised.

At this point, a couple of things may happen. The change is dropped or there is an agreement to pilot it somewhere in the organization. Another possibility is that the most senior person will make a decision to move forward with the change. This decision is usually faced with unenthusiastic support and a general agreement to give it a try with few, if any, tangible commitments made to it.

Discussion on how much the change will cost may also take place. Early in the change process, an effort is made to calculate the ROI for the change. Whether the change is internally supported or by an outside vendor or consultant, the cost is typically understated.

If done internally, cost can be either under- or overstated because the internal people either don't understand the details of what it will take to implement the change or they don't comprehend the real effect of the change effort on the organization's resources. If done using external sources, such as a consultant, then this understatement is both a function of their unfamiliarity with your organization and the self-serving need to win your business.

Either analysis can also be affected by internal politics. The organizational position and importance of the person leading the change can have a huge impact on the prediction of cost.

There may also be discussions about the type and amount of change expected. This conversation typically focuses on what was observed in other organizations or is based on the results promised by an external consultant. There is a vague idea that the organization needs to change but it is often no more specific than a "we want some of that" idea.

WHY IS THE CHANGE IMPORTANT TO SENIOR EXECUTIVE LEADERSHIP?

The organization's leadership needs to clearly and unequivocally express why the change is important to them personally. A concise, consistent message delivered over an extended period of time and through different communication methods is a necessary component of organization change. The extended period of time ends only when there is clear evidence that the change has been fully deployed and is producing the intended results. The pattern of this communication is like a *V*, starting small and broadening over time across more and more of the organization. It starts with the senior executive leader's direct reports during the start-up of the change deployment and broadens across the organization at a pace that mirrors the progress of the change so that people are told what has been done, not what will be done. This "do and tell" approach will be discussed later during the communication planning section of the book.

This communication by the leadership convinces people that devoting time and energy to the effort will make a difference to the organization, its customers, and the individual. A concise message is repeated not only by the leader, but also by other members of the chain of command.

Leaders up and down the chain of command have only so much management capital to spend. If the change message is complex, unsustainable, and unbelievable, it is unlikely that it will be communicated throughout the whole organization. There are too many other day-to-day issues and problems requiring the subordinate leadership's attention. Furthermore, these daily issues directly impact the short-term results that are required from the lower-level leadership. These daily issues will have more effect on the lower-level leadership's personal performance rating and ability to hold onto their role and make a living. As a result, these daily tasks get more attention from the lower-level leadership.

Developing a consistent message is not complex, but neither is it necessarily easy. The starting point is the fundamental success measure (or goal) of the organization. If the organization is a publicly traded company, then the likely purpose of the change is to increase revenue, profitability, and product quality. If the organization is a non-profit, the purpose of the change will be directly connected to the mission of the organization. The only credible reason for a senior executive leader to want change is that it will have a direct effect on the organizational goals for which the senior executive leader is directly responsible. The best messages are created with few words, are easy to remember, and evoke a vivid image that connected to the basic purpose of the organization. A few corporate examples illustrate this point. Jack Welch's message to GE was that they would be first or second in the market or they would not be in that market. At Cummins, we said Six Sigma would be used to continuously improve products toward perfection. And at Apple, Steve Jobs led the company to unparalleled success based on this philosophy: "If you keep your eye on the profit, you're going to skimp on the product. But if you focus on making really great products, then the profits will follow."

The senior executive leader communicates this message over and over and over and, yes, over again. He or she becomes the champion for the change. During speeches, formal and informal company gatherings, visits to different parts of the company, staff meetings, investor/analyst meetings, interviews, in the annual report and any other place where groups are gathered and the organization's leader is speaking, writing, blogging or otherwise communicating, the message is repeated. Further, the message is communicated over a series of years until it is clear that the change is part of the structural fabric of the organization and that the desired results are occurring. This connection of communication to results is a key element of the change effort and is necessary to ensure that people "get it" and are doing the work that the change requires. This is the only way people will believe that the change is serious and won't go away.

WHY IS IT IMPORTANT TO ME?

Making the change important to the individual sub-unit leader is the job of senior executive leadership. If the change isn't important to the individual sub-unit leader, he or she will at best be disinterested and at worst resistant or hostile. This is best thought of as a cascade through the first few levels of the organization. The CEO (or most senior executive of the organization) owns the responsibility to explain why this change is important for the company and for his/her direct reports. The senior executive leader describes for other executives and managers:

- Why this specific change is important
- The specific problem that this change is meant to address
- Why he/she became convinced this is the right change to make
- What this change will mean to the organization (What are the organizational measures that will improve because of the change?)
- What the expectations are for each individual in the senior executive leadership group
- The consequences of not getting on board and actively driving the change in the organization
- The performance targets:
  - For business the measure is cost reduction, margin improvement, profit growth, revenue growth, and so on
  - For non-profits, the measures could include numbers of people served, donor population growth, volunteer increases, and so on
- Clarity regarding the leader's openness to discussion about *how* to make the change, though the change itself is not open to debate

Each sub-unit leader is responsible for the same communication to their direct reports. This continues as a cascade through the leadership ranks.

It is critically important that you as a sub-unit leader not communicate to your own direct reports until you yourself truly believe what you are going to tell them. If you don't, they will quickly know you don't mean it and this by itself can doom a change effort.

HOW ARE WE GOING TO GET THERE?

What am I (the sub-unit leader) supposed to do?

Leaders in the business want to understand their role and their work. Communicating specific actions is critical to this understanding and the change effort. A Goal Tree is a useful tool for accomplishing this task. The Goal Tree is a simple structure for showing various work expectations that are connected to the most important goals of the organization. Its creation clarifies tasks from the top to the bottom of the organization.

The Goal Tree (Figure 4.1) is made up of the short- to medium-term (three to five year) initiatives and projects (six months to a year) needed to drive the organization toward the future state. This is a simplified version

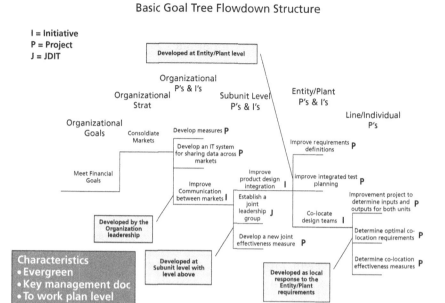

Figure 4.1 Basic Goal Tree flowdown structure.

of Hoshin Planning or Policy Deployment (developed by Yoji Akao in Japan in the 1980s). In the Seven Management Planning Tools, the Goal Tree is called a Structure Tree. Forms of this tool are used in various ways.

A Goal Tree is used to connect the improvement work that is needed throughout the levels of the organization to the top-level goals and objectives derived from the future state. The Goal Tree helps to create context for people in the organization and gives leadership a document for discussing where the organization is going. The document also shows people how their work contributes to the overall success of the organization.

The development of the Goal Tree is a top-down, iterative effort. It requires a joint planning session between adjacent levels of the organization matching resources to goals, objectives, and projects, driving to agreement regarding what work will be done. In Hoshin Planning this is known as "catch-ball." The intent is that the Goal Tree is a product of negotiated give-and-take between the various levels regarding work to be done and resources deployed to do it.

Goals and objectives drive strategies. Strategies beget initiatives and projects in a continuous chain down to the lowest level of the organization capable of completing improvement projects. The Goal Tree illustration (Figure 4.1) shows a model of how this process works.

Key to its success is the communication that happens between the levels. The Seven Management Planning Tools are effective for enabling this planning session.

Regarding the Seven Management Planning Tools, in 1976, the Union of Japanese Scientists and Engineers (JUSE) saw the need for tools to promote innovation, communicate information, and successfully plan major projects. A team researched and developed seven new quality control tools, often called the Seven Management and Planning Tools, or simply the Seven Management Tools. Not all the tools were new, but their collection and promotion as a set of tools was. These tools are especially suited to helping a group work through actions required and in what order.

CREATING A GOAL TREE

Vision and Mission

The first, most important step to creating a Goal Tree is to decide on the organization's overall direction. This starts with the development of a vision and mission (these are summary statements of the future state described earlier) for the organization. This is an important first step because without a vision and mission, the Goal Tree process is directionless.

The vision and mission are the highest-level descriptions of organizational aspiration and are important for communicating what the organization is about and where it is headed. The vision and mission are long range (> ten years) and are meant to be compelling descriptions of the future. There are ample books, articles, and consultants that describe how to do this, so it will not be covered here.

The Goal Tree is comprised of four basic elements: Goals, Strategies, Initiatives, and Projects. The pattern used to construct the Goal Tree is a set of "what-how" relationships. The goals define what we want to be or what we want to achieve; the strategy describes how we will accomplish this goal. The strategy becomes a *what* and the initiatives describe *how* we will accomplish this strategy. The initiatives then become the *what* and the projects become *how we will accomplish the initiatives*. This pattern is shown in Figure 4.1.

Goals

Goals are developed from the vision, mission, and future state. What does the organization need to do to progress toward the future? The goals, like the vision, mission, and future state, come from the organization's leadership and are best accomplished when limited to three to five. More than five seems overwhelming for many organizations and even setting five goals is a stretch for some. A number of questions help development of the goals:

- Where are we now?
- What is most important to our customers?
- What is most important to the organization?
- What is most important to the people of the organization?
- Who are the other critical stakeholders and what is most important to them?
- What are the key drivers of our future?
- What measures will monitor progress toward the goals?

A tool that the organization's leadership can use to develop the goal, initiatives, and projects is the Affinity Diagram (from the Seven Management Planning Tools) or the KJ process (named for its inventor, Jiro Kawakita). The Affinity Diagram/KJ Process is driven by the answer to the question: "What are all the things we need to do to accomplish our vision, mission, and future state?" The answers to the questions are organized into groups of common ideas. This sorting identifies the basic buckets of work that are needed to accomplish the future state. Many things drive the development of the affinity diagram:

- Leadership knowledge
- Market research
- Customer feedback
- Technology changes
- Future product plans
- Future market plans
- Growth projections
- Government requirements rules and laws
- Input from the people of the organization
- Supplier feedback
- Current problems, issues and improvements

Strategies

If the goals define *what* the organization needs to do, strategies describe *how* the organization will get there. Given that this process is taking place at the highest level of the organization, the strategies are also high-level, broad-based descriptions of the key things to pursue on the way to the goals. Strategies tend to have a five to ten year time horizon.

Initiatives

Initiatives are the larger groupings of actions that must be taken to accomplish the strategies. The timeframe of initiatives tends to be three to five years, although it could be longer or shorter.

Projects

Projects are what need to be done to accomplish the initiatives. They are focused activities, led by a project leader and supported by knowledgeable team members. Projects are time-bound, and scoped for completion within three to 12 months.

WHAT ARE YOU GOING TO DO TO HELP ME?

This is basic to the change effort. Questions requiring answers include:

- Whose budget, corporate or local, pays for the change costs (training, travel, computers/software, books, consultants, and so on)?

- Are new skills required for the change? How are the skills acquired? Who is accountable for making sure the skills are developed?

- Does the change require adding people? How many and where? Are these additions added to staff that are already in the organization? To whom will the new people report? How will their budget be established?

- Is there anything that we will stop doing?

- How will we measure progress? What is the process for measuring? What are the measurement definitions? Where is measurement data stored?

- Is money available to reward outstanding performance (for instance, bonuses, incentive awards, trophies, and so on)?

WHAT'S MY INCENTIVE?

What is the reward for excellent performance? Can everyone achieve excellence or is this a "best of the best" approach with winners and losers? These are decisions to be made by leadership and are consistent with the organization's culture. Defining the recognition process is an element of creating accountability and reinforcing the change up and down the organizational hierarchy. People need to know what is expected of them. Recognition of both acceptable and unacceptable behavior defines the boundaries and makes it clear to people what the organizational norms are.

What is the consequence for failing to achieve a required level of performance? Defining consequences for failure is a very difficult task. It is important to connect negative consequences with the organization's culture. The two ends of the cultural spectrum are authoritarian and relationship-based. In a culture that tends to be top down and authoritarian, punishment for poor performance is more common. Therefore, setting standards, enforcing them, and punishing those who don't comply is expected and consistent with the way the organization operates.

In a culture that is more relationship-based, punishment tends to be more difficult to both administer and maintain over time. People have closer personal relationships, which makes holding each other accountable and administering organizational discipline much more difficult. In this culture, positive incentive and personal appeal for support tends to work best.

Cultures that are somewhere between these two extremes (probably most organizations) will blend reward and punishment in a way that can be consistently applied and, therefore, seen as enduring through the change.

It is important to have a plan that is consistent with the organizational culture; otherwise, both sanction and reward systems will do more harm than good and result in general cynicism and even fear regarding future change efforts.

5

Making Change and the Role of the Consultant

An organization can benefit from using consultants who come with specialized knowledge and skills. It is extremely important that the consulting relationship is managed like any other supplier. Understanding the consultant's capabilities, establishing clear deliverables, measures, and timeframe are all critical elements of successfully engaging a consultant to assist the change process.

The best consulting contract I experienced was for an initial Six Sigma program start-up. The consulting group contracted with the company to deliver knowledge over a two-year period. There were clear up-front costs and a defined time period for the engagement. We picked the first training consultants, established objective measures of performance, and connected them to an incentive component of the contract. The consultant helped us meet our contractual commitment to develop the capability to lead the effort following the consultants' departure. The relationship was not without occasional conflicts, but both the consultants and the company lived up to the commitments made, resulting in a very successful start-up of Six Sigma as well as an enduring program that spanned the better part of two decades. Later, we followed the same basic approach with other consultants that we employed, most notably for supply chain improvement.

THE CONSULTING CONTRACT

The general timeline for the elements of the consulting contract includes:

- Making the decision to engage a consultant
- Benchmarking, comparing, and selecting a consulting firm
- Scoping, defining, and agreeing to a specific consulting contract with specific deliverables
- Beginning the engagement
- Monitoring and reviewing progress

- Concluding the original contract following accomplishment of deliverables

- Following-up with the consultant informally as necessary and/or

- Developing a new contract with deliverables as required

Following the formal close of the contract with the consultant, often the relationship needs to continue. This can be formal, informal, or both. It is a decision to be made based on the needs of the organization.

This decision to hire a consultant is driven by a number of factors including:

- Leadership wants the change effort to begin as soon as possible

- Making a significant change in a big organization requires talented people

- Another organization successfully employed a specific consultant

Leadership wants the change effort to begin as soon as possible. The consulting group has a methodology, training materials that can be tailored (or not), and experienced consultants who are ready to go. The organization will change faster if there is no need to devote time and effort developing and managing an internally created training program. The consultants can help the organization fast track the implementation if their offering is clearly connected to the future state.

Making a significant change in a complex organization requires talented people. Typically, the best people in the organization are already over-committed to other important activities so they can't immediately absorb additional responsibilities. Something as important as changing corporate culture shouldn't be given to anyone other than the organization's best people; others are not as likely to do it right and typically lack the political influence necessary to lead the change. In the end, the organization will end up wasting time and money if the best people are not leading the change initiative.

Hiring a consultant can provide an infusion of highly-competent people to allow the organization time to decide who the right people are internally to lead the change over the long haul and to free them from other duties. It is important to include this transition in the overall plan. The change ultimately has to be owned by people in the organization or it will eventually fail.

Another organization successfully employed a specific consultant. Effective consultants have a track record of success. The perception among some executives is that if their organization just copies what someone else did, everything will be great. However, the "one-size-fits-all" approach can be problematic. Organizations simply are not the same. Consultants might make marginal changes to their standard approach to show that they are sensitive to the needs of the new organization but, at its heart, the approach is the same. To be fair to the consultants, this is what they do. They know they have a limited amount of time to influence organizational change. The consultant honestly believes that success can be repeated if the new organization follows the prescription it is handed. However, it is not the same organization as the last one. In fact, almost everything is different. Marginal changes typically don't work and the result can be another failed "program of the month." Therefore, monitoring the consultant's processes takes on added importance to avoid this pitfall.

To make sure the consultant delivers what the organization needs, it is important to conduct the contracting process between the organization and a consultant with the same rigor that is applied to any other supplier contract. I have seen this step missed when an understanding existed between the leader of the organization and the leader of the consulting firm. There was a feeling that they could trust one another to do the right thing. The standard kinds of negotiations that are conducted with suppliers were ignored because the personal relationships were already established and so negotiation was unnecessary. After all, they are selling great ideas. It is really hard to haggle over money in the face of great ideas.

A good consulting contract will include some risk to the consultant should the change effort fall short. It will also include clear measures of success. It is a mistake for the consultant to face no penalty, beyond reputation, for a failure to deliver impactful change as spelled out in the deliverables of the contract.

Interview the consultant(s) who will initially be doing the work of the contract. These initial consultants will set the tone of the relationship and it is important to know who will be working with the organization's people. To the extent possible, find a time to see them in action. This won't prevent all possible problems, but it will help to eliminate some avoidable mistakes with consultants who are a poor fit for your organization. The reality is that consulting organizations typically sell themselves with their best, most experienced people. Often somebody on the senior staff of the organization knows the principle consultant, or knows somebody who does, and has given the consulting group glowing reviews. It's not until the contract is signed and the work begins that the consulting firm's operational people show up. These are the consultants who will develop and guide the change in the organization. In my experience, consultants tend to fit one of five basic profiles.

THE KINDS OF PEOPLE YOU WANT (AND DON'T WANT)

Make sure to get precisely the kinds of people from the consulting firm you want working with the people in your organization.

Figure 5.1 The Superstar.

The Superstar: This is the consultant you want to work with (Fig. 5.1). These consultants do their homework and show up prepared. They know about the organization and have asked to interview key leaders before they begin any work. They take time to tailor the training material with real world examples that are meaningful to your organization. Easy to work with, they know how to develop relationships and to influence and persuade others. They are typically fabulous communicators who show up ready to help solve your problems. You can call them any time and you will want to stay in touch with them long after the consulting contract has ended because they have proven their worth.

I have been fortunate to work with a few consultants of this type during my years in the corporate world. They are rare finds and many of them end up back in the corporate world leading organizations. The first Six Sigma consultants we used for our Six Sigma launch were handpicked because of their approach and attitude. They were a perfect fit for our company. This ended up being one of the keys to our early Six Sigma success. As the relationship expanded, we also had a few problem consultants from the same firm. So it is important to recognize that active monitoring of the consulting group is an on-going responsibility of the hiring organization.

Figure 5.2 The Gray Hair.

The Gray Hair: This person has been in the work world for thirty or forty years (Fig. 5.2). These people have tons of experience and may have decided it was time to leave the world of day-to-day operations and help other people do what they have done. The other possibility is that this person is a displaced worker who is looking for another full-time position. Gray haired consultants know a lot!

However, they often learned through the school of hard knocks. They learned by doing as well as by following and leading others. This doesn't always translate into the capability to coach and develop others, particularly when the consultant has no real stake in the success of the organization.

Usually all this consultant knows is based on personally taking charge, stepping up to be accountable, making decisions on the fly, and being a good leader. This style of knowledge may not be easily transferable to other workers.

The MBA: This person tends to be in the 25 to 35 year old age group and often has never really done anything more than study theory in school (Fig. 5.3). These people have learned the process that the consulting agency is selling. They are bright and eager. But, they don't know how to lead change because they have never done it.

Often they are consulting to gain experience before moving into the business world themselves. It is hard for them to understand how people feel about the changes being made because they have never actually lived through any complex change. They are all about dollars and cents, headcount, restructuring, and eliminating non-value added work without really understanding how these terms relate to what the organization does or the effect of this type of change on the organization's people.

Figure 5.3 The MBA.

The Good Guy: This is a really likable person but not someone you would hire to lead your own company (Fig. 5.4). He or she has sufficient middle management experience and skill to be competent in a structured setting, but has little sense of how to help an organization unfamiliar to them.

They have never seen and don't know the people, products, or processes. They tend to get lost in a hurry and quickly lose the confidence of the people they are directly trying to help. But because everybody likes them personally, often executive leadership doesn't learn, in a timely way, that the Good Guy isn't that effective. Another factor hindering executive leadership's awareness of this problem is that people believe it to be political suicide to speak up. They definitely do not want to be perceived as against the change. So, they go along with what is happening to stay out of trouble especially when the consultants are good guys that everybody likes.

Figure 5.4 The Good Guy.

The Dud: This consultant shows up with a big ego and a know-it-all attitude (Fig. 5.5). This type of consultant quickly alienates the people they are supposed to guide. Often these

Figure 5.5 The Dud.

consultants are inexperienced and have no idea how to build relationships with the people they are supposed to help.

Another Dud type of consultant is the nice person who just doesn't know what needs to be done or the nice, inexperienced consultant who doesn't have the necessary skill set to be effective. The Dud is probably the most destructive consultant type because they can poison the change for everyone.

We experienced this at Cummins when, after a few months in the engagement, the consulting firm sent a new consultant to lead a training launch for an administrative group. This consultant was clearly an enthusiastic expert, but had no experience consulting. A favorite phrase was, "We did this at Company X"; utterances that continued even after repeated advice to stop. Additionally, all of the examples this consultant used were from working at this one other company. Some of this is expected, but the consultant failed to understand the audience or to listen when given guidance to soften this approach. Making matters worse was that the consultant was arrogant and demeaning to people. The consulting firm was eventually asked to withdraw this particular consultant from the engagement. But this left behind a negative image with the administrative groups, which took time and effort to overcome.

A risk to consider when hiring consultants is that bringing somebody in can play into the hands of the people who don't want to make the change in the first place. They have seen this scenario played out before. Consultants don't know who the key players are. They don't know how things work in the organization. Consultants have no real authority even if they are working for the CEO. This can turn into a classic "trade space for time" strategy by those who are negative about the change.

A historical illustration of this "trade space for time" strategy is the Russian response to Napoleon's invasion of Russia in the 1800s. As Napoleon advanced, the Russians pulled back, burning the ground as they went, and leaving the French with nothing to eat. The Russians knew that winter would be more destructive to the French than any Russian assault and so they waited, trading space for time. The Russians ultimately drove Napoleon and his powerful army out of Russia in what became one of the bloodiest retreats in military history.

Anti-change people know that if they are patient, doing the minimum necessary to look like they are supportive, the consultants will eventually leave because of frustration and with a false claim of success or else a lack of real change that leads to a termination of the consultant's contract. The anti-change people have traded space for time to thwart the change.

Hiring a consultant to help kick-start a change can be beneficial. The process needs to be closely monitored like any other. Assuming a decision has been made to engage a consultant, what's next? The next chapter addresses ways to make a consulting engagement effective.

6

Making the Consulting Engagement Effective

Once the decision is made to use a consulting firm, the organization has to make the partnership work. What follows are a few more lessons that should be considered when specifying particulars of the consulting relationship, scope, and expectations.

The future state defines the change the organization is making. Ensure that any training purchased from a consultant is clearly linked to the future state of the change. Make sure the training that is offered meets your organization's needs.

This clarity is important because some consultants will recommend tracking the organizational activities as the measure of consultant effectiveness. The consultant will also make recommendations detailing what the organization's employees are supposed to do. The organization's performance is then tracked using a scorecard built around the major elements of the consultant's plan. People in your organization are assigned to collect data and create reports. The data collected for measurement are based on activities performed (that is, numbers of people trained, active projects, and so on). This data is sent to be aggregated by corporate people who tend to be at some distance from the activity and lack practical or contextual understanding of what is really happening. The consultant then analyzes the reports and helps senior executive leadership assess conformity to the consultant's plan. With a lack of understanding and connection to the goals and objectives of the organization, this counting exercise ultimately provides little benefit to the organization or its customers.

Effectiveness measures based on activity are important in the very beginning of a change effort, but have to quickly mature to reflect customer and organizational success (more on this during the discussion of S-Curves).

If the consulting group's involvement with the company is long-term, measurement of business metric improvements may eventually become part of regular reporting. Unfortunately, the consulting group is usually long gone before any business or customer impacts are seen. The consultant's involvement is usually short-term because the cost of keeping the consultant under contract for a significant period is prohibitive. Also, the consultant's business model may require that the consultant move on to the next contract. Therefore, establishing this linkage and measurement during the contracting phase makes the purpose of the training clear and answers people's need to know what they are being asked to do and why.

The cost of a consultant often doesn't end when the contract period is completed. When working with a consultant who is offering training as part of the engagement, the organization is contractually obligated to the consulting group to pay for each training event. Typically, this often means an initial licensing fee for the consultant's intellectual property, a per day rate for each consultant, and all travel expenses.

The training tends to be generic to the consultant's methodology and processes. It is rarely in the language of the customer organization because there is a big charge for customizing training material. Customizing the training will also delay the implementation of the planned change. With customization, the implementation time is lengthened because the consultant doesn't really know the company and people have to be assigned to help with cultural nomenclature. Further, customization can make it difficult to incorporate potential future upgrades, especially when any vendor software supports the training. The consultant will be available to help and support the organization for a fee as needed changes are discovered. Therefore, before starting down the training path, it is important to select a consultant whose methodology is aligned to the expected change to minimize both time and costs.

Leadership accountability for delivering organizational results can often conflict with the consultant's plans. The various levels of leadership are accountable and rewarded for how well they deliver the organization's products and services. Senior executive leadership will often layer on the additional accountability for delivery to the consultant's plan without consideration for the impact on day-to-day deliverables or making it a formal part of the lower level work plans. This can lead to tension as the leadership struggles to balance the two priorities.

In addition, the further from the organization's center (headquarters), the less compliant leaders tend to be with senior executive leadership mandates that conflict with basic deliverables. The farther away one gets from the organization's headquarters, the easier it is to do the bare minimum to comply without really doing the necessary work. Many mid-level people will take a wait-and-see attitude to new initiatives because they assume that while there may be an initial push when the new initiative is first announced, it is likely that the initiative will soon lose momentum. The middle level leaders believe that if they are patient, a new initiative will soon take the place of the most recent change effort, so there is little point in wasting time and effort working on something that didn't really matter after all.

An example of this phenomenon comes from my days as a fleet and distribution manager in the late 1980s. A colleague and I were assigned the task of developing new delivery processes that were to be implemented across the company. We spent months researching, experimenting, designing, and developing processes as well as writing and publishing our results. We presented our results and the mandate was given to implement the work. We printed copies of our plan and sent them to our peers across the company and while there was some initial tracking, the momentum slowed. It wasn't long before senior executive leadership lost interest and we soon moved on to the next idea. While this is not specifically a consulting example, it is illustrative of how changes lose energy. (I recently found a copy of the implementation guides that we had developed and it made me wonder if other copies were sitting on shelves collecting dust just as mine was. It was just another corporate change mandate that failed to produce results.)

With the departure of the consulting group, new staff groups need to be established to carry on the work. Often the process run by the consulting group will include a hand-off plan. This is intended to smooth the organization's transition from working with the consultants to working with the new staff group. This hand-off plan will entail training internal people to be experts in the consultant's methodology, processes, and tools as well as training staff to take on new roles and responsibilities. Without in-house experts, it will be very difficult to sustain the changes and improvements. The consultant will typically offer training for the internal subject-matter experts and the staff for a fee.

Selecting the right people to do the work internally is difficult. It may be difficult to decide whom to put in the new expert roles. The recommendation from the consulting group is to select the organization's most promising future leaders. This shows commitment to the change, puts the best implementers on the front line of the change, and creates confidence that this can really work. However, there is a variable response from the organization because they know that trouble comes their way when failing to accomplish the organization's primary mission already led by their best people. The change is often perceived as disruptive to the main mission. The best people don't have the time to participate in train-the-trainer sessions and to lead others through training. They might also be unavailable due to their valued relationship with an important customer, their specialized technical or work knowledge, or they may prefer to stay in their current job hoping to move to a new leadership position where they are.

This narrows the pool of candidates. For many mid-level organizations, their contribution is the person or people that they can most easily spare. From the beginning, people in the organization suspect that their direct leadership doesn't really support the change and the people assigned to help implement it are tangible evidence that their suspicions are correct. These change leaders aren't bad people, but they are not the people who would normally be assigned to the highest priority of the organization. This creates another barrier to broad-based support and participation in the change effort suffers. To avoid this problem, senior executive leadership involvement in the selection of the first cadre of subject matter experts is important.

Senior executive leadership impatience grows as the clock ticks forward and meaningful change has not occurred. In a complex organization, the effort to start a change initiative takes time. Hiring the consulting group, developing a plan, getting the consultant(s) onboard, selecting people to attend training, scheduling the training, enrolling key leaders, developing data collection and tracking systems, plus myriad other details all absorb real clock time. Often, it can be six months or longer before anything begins to happen. During this time, many key leaders of the organization will become impatient with a lack of results. Others will start to lose interest as time and the needs of the organization continue to move forward diverting their attention from the change effort.

Additionally, at the mid-level, personnel turnover is taking place and every new person comes with a slowdown in implementation. By the end of the first year, the effort is struggling. By the end of the second year, evidence of the change effort is visible in only a few areas. By the end of the third year, the three ring binders used to implement the change are sitting on shelves around the organization and the software that was installed sits forgotten and unused on the organization's network and hard drives.

Exasperation with the pace of change is a reflection of a leadership group that is used to getting things done, often by force of personal involvement and direction. But, the leadership required for specific, focused, deliverable-oriented tasks is very different from the leadership required to employ consultants to initiate broad-based, systemic changes. This kind of leadership is more influence-based than action-based. It uses a different set of leadership skills. It requires setting direction, goals, and measures, holding outsiders (the consultants) accountable, coaching and mentoring of subordinates, real-time correction and redirection, and most of all, communication, communication, communication. These tasks require a sense of patient perseverance. Many senior executive leaders have never had to exercise these skills and may not actually possess them. Their exasperation results in a turning away from the change effort and moving on to the next great idea that is intended to make the organization better.

SELECTING A CONSULTANT

Unsuccessfully implementing a new change initiative is rarely a complete failure. People learn new skills and are exposed to new methodologies. A new sense of purpose connected with the change effort can occur among the senior executive leadership. A few new tools or processes may have been introduced that survive and become broadly used. But, generally, the change doesn't penetrate very deeply into the soul and culture of the organization. After a few years, sometimes only months, very few people even remember that there was a change effort, let alone what the change was supposed to produce.

What happens next is predictable. Personnel change positions, new needs and requirements arise, and a desire to make the organization better results in the identification of the next great idea. And the cycle begins again.

Hiring consultants to assist in a change effort has its place, especially when the consultant possesses specialized knowledge that the organization needs, and hiring consultants is the quickest way to get that knowledge. Conducting a consulting assessment prior to starting the change effort can make the consulting arrangement more effective. The consulting assessment includes, but is not limited to, the following questions:

- Why do you need to change? (competition, new markets, new businesses, significant growth, and so on)

- What are the change goals and objectives? What measures are you trying to affect with your change?

- Based on research and benchmarking, what skills and/or knowledge are lacking in your organization?

- Why do you think you need a consultant instead of permanently hiring people who possess the necessary skills?

- What role do you want the consultant to play? Are they transferring knowledge? Delivering a specific result? Delivering an engineering solution?

- Who are the viable consulting candidates? What process will you use for selecting the best candidate?

- Who are the references for the consultants being considered? What do they say about the consulting candidates? What are the positives and negatives? Set up a benchmarking visit to see the consultant in action and the longer term results of the consultant's work.

- What approaches do the consultants use to drive change? How do these approaches fit with the organization's culture?

- What timeline do the different consultants use for deployment of the change?

- Who are the consultants who will lead the engagement? See the assigned consultants in action. Do they fit with your organization's culture? How long can the consulting group commit to keeping these consultants on your account?

- What do you want to include in the supplier contract?

    1. What is the total cost of the engagement?

    2. What are the expectations of the consultant?

    3. What penalty clauses are the consultants willing to accept in the contract?

    4. What additional incentives do you want to build into the contract for consultant performance beyond the basic agreement?

    5. What commitments must be made by your organization for successful change?

    6. What additional charges can you expect to incur during the engagement? What would trigger these costs?

Consultants have their place and can be very beneficial to a change effort. But, they have to be managed. The information in this chapter, while by no means exhaustive, is meant to help you think about a consulting engagement and how to manage it.

7

The S-Curves

A difficulty experienced by senior executive leadership is keeping expectations in line with the real pace of change. Change almost always takes longer than expected for several reasons and in larger organizations these reasons are magnified. Some of those reasons include but are not limited to:

- Complications arising from communication of the change and what is expected

- Distance from the organization's home base where the change originates

- The number of people to enroll and engage in the change process

- Cultural differences across the organization that can mute or even conflict with the desired change

- Problems with language differences and varying interpretations as to which direction to go

HOW CHANGE OCCURS

The development of S-Curves (also called maturity curves) (Figure 7.1) is an approach that can help to define and manage how a change will occur and recognizes the time element of change in a structured way. The S-Curves define the phases of change over time in active terms that paint a word picture of where the organization is going and how it will get there. S-Curves also act as a communication tool that shows people what to expect as the change is made. They also counteract one barrier that often impedes change. That barrier is the natural impulse of leadership to be impatient and seek the end result NOW! The development of a set of agreed S-Curves can help address this desire.

Maturity growth is another way to think about S-Curves. I have seen S-Curves or maturity curves used in TRIZ (the Theory of Inventive Problem Solving). But I was first introduced to them after a friend came back from a visit to Massachusetts Institute of Technology (MIT). The basic idea in S-Curves is that there is a separation between today's

How change occurs

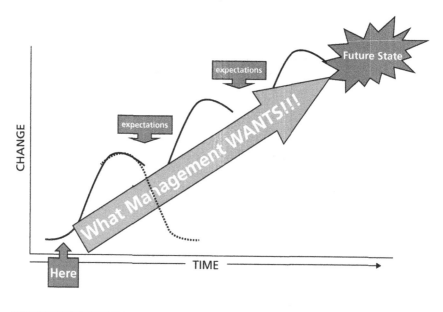

Figure 7.1 The development of S-Curves.

performance and the desired performance described in the future state. The organization will progress through a series of system changes (maturity) on the way to realizing the future state. These changes are the S-Curves. At the top of each S-Curve is a sub-goal and a set of measures that are connected to the future state. These sub-goals and performance measures are the control mechanisms for senior executive leadership as progress is made from S to S. This helps leadership to visualize that the future state can only be achieved over time and through a connected series of sub-goals and evolving measures.

The development of S-Curves also helps to keep progress moving forward. The temptation is to stop when a sub-goal is reached and declare victory because it is here that real success is visible, often for the first time. Emotionally, it feels like something has been accomplished when, in fact, it is only one milestone on the path to the future state.

It is also important to notice that the S-Curve is just the left side of a bell-shaped curve. If the organization tries to stop the change process and hold on to the gains that have been made at the top of the curve, the gain will eventually atrophy and decay. The progress made will be lost. This is because organizations are living entities and living things need to grow and change or they decay and die. S-Curves are a mechanism to manage growth and change over time.

I briefly discussed the future state in Chapter 2. The future state describes what leadership wants the organization to look like following the change. It is, by definition, different than the organization of today.

Think about your last vacation. Did you just jump in the car and take off? Likely not (excepting the truly adventurous reader who thinks unplanned road trips are the height of fun) because most of us want to know things such as cost, weather, distance, activities, and so on. So, the simple vacation begins with an idea of where to go. Even if the vacation is a stay-at-home vacation that, too, describes a destination. Everything else that one does to prepare for the vacation is driven by that one decision, which is a future state.

An organization is no different. What is the organization to be? What will people do? What will be going on in the organization's future? Answers to these and other questions give people in the organization direction and helps them to know what improvements to make on the way to achieving the future state.

One caveat here is that the future state is not an absolute. A future state is a potential destination that is flexible to a changing environment and new knowledge. This is the future state's role as part of the S-Curves. S-Curves allow for changes to be made to the future state, to intermediate goals and objectives as new things are learned and reality impacts the changes that are made. A future state is *not* meant to be an inviolable statement of what the organization will unequivocally be at some distant point in time. It *is* based on what we know today and is used to start an organization's change journey.

STARTING POINT, FUTURE STATE AND AN ORGANIZATION'S PURPOSE

The starting point of a future state is the organization's vision, its mission, and its values. These elements define what the organization stands for compared to other similar organizations as well as the greater society. The future state must be consistent with the vision, mission, and values. For this book, it is assumed that the vision, mission, and values already exist. If not, they need to be created.

The future state answers the basic question, "If we took the top off of the organization five years from now, what do we want to see? If our change is successful and everything is operating perfectly, what will we see?" Once the required change has been decided, the future state is developed based on the answers to some key questions. These questions include:

- How will the change affect customers? What will customers be doing? How will we be perceived in the marketplace? How will we treat our customers?

- How will the change affect the organization's people? How will the organization's people behave? What is the organizational environment in which they work?

- How will the change affect leadership? What will we see leadership doing?

- How will the change affect suppliers? How will we behave with our suppliers?

- What processes will be affected by the change? What will be different about these processes?

- How will we measure our organization's success? How will we measure the success of the change?

These and other questions help to structure a behavior-based word picture of the future that can be communicated and refined as new things are learned about where the organization needs to go.

AFFINITY DIAGRAMS OR KJ PROCESSES

As each question (and others) is answered, individual responses are placed on a separate sticky note. The answers to these questions and other ideas can then be sorted using an affinity diagram or KJ process. The affinity diagram/KJ process forms the foundation of a behavior-based future state and serves as a communication vehicle to people in the organization.

The affinity/KJ diagram is the basis of a written document that is the organizational future state. The goal is to make sure all members of the organization understand the overall direction and what success actually looks like. This becomes a shared vision of the future. All improvement work then becomes a step along the path to achievement of this shared vision.

It is important to remember that this future state is not an unalterable description. The future state is reviewed on a recurring basis. At a minimum, this review should occur annually.

As new things are learned, the direction is modified to reflect this new understanding. The key to the future state's value is its use as a communication vehicle for the members of the organization; therefore it has to be believable.

Following the development of the future state, the next step in the development of the S-Curves is always the current state (where you are now). Developing the current state is an assessment of where you are today. The Baldrige Criteria is an excellent tool for understanding where the organization is now.

Now that the ends of the model have been created, each S-Curve is described in behavioral terms. What do you expect to see in each phase? The first S-Curve is often a period of time when research, consultant advice, executive education, definition development, basic training, project planning, and structured project management takes place. These tend to be transactional activities having a yes/no, "we did it or did not do it" character. There are a number of common activities that can be seen in the first S-Curve. These characteristics typically include but are not limited to the following:

- Choosing a leader
- Developing a leadership review process
- Selecting a project team
- Deciding whether or not to use a consultant
- Choosing a methodology
- Training people
- Selecting business measures of success
- Agreeing to resource allocation
- Defining the roles of the different levels of leadership

The work of each S-Curve has a different character and can best be seen in the definition of the goal and measures for each curve with the expected behaviors and interactions becoming more complex along the path to the future state.

As progress is being made to the top of one S-Curve, planning begins for the next. The mission is to leap the gap between the curves with minimal decline and begin quickly progressing toward the next sub-goal. With each S-Curve the organization improves its capability to perform the increasingly complex tasks of more a mature organization. This process continues until the future state is achieved.

USING S-CURVES TO MAKE FORWARD PROGRESS

In reality, as progress is made, the future state is upgraded. If the future state is stated broadly enough, progress up the S-Curves to the future state can take a very long time. When the future state is achieved, a new future state is created for the next change effort and the process begins again.

There are a number of benefits to this approach:

- There is a real sense of progress that keeps people working toward the future state.

- There is a clear understanding and expectation for how long real change takes and how much effort is involved. Large-scale change can't be taken on lightly without a clear understanding of the resources and the time required for the on-going planning, execution and reviews that are necessary.

- S-Curves allow the various parts of the organization to be in different places along the change journey. In a complex organization, this is simply a reality. Recognizing this reality reduces the frustration that comes with trying to force all organizational elements to move together in lockstep when some parts are not ready and others are well beyond the stated requirement. The only "must" is that continuous improvement toward the future state be planned and delivered. Each organization will have a different set of planned actions because they are in different places along the S-Curves. But all organizations will be moving toward the same ultimate objective.

- The S-Curves can become a communication tool for understanding where things stand and where they are going. This will enhance the alignment of improvement work.

- S-Curves also align leadership expectations to the real pace of change. This is no small challenge. As discussed earlier, leadership impatience can get in the way of real progress and may be replaced with the false progress of telling and showing senior executive leadership what they want to hear instead of the reality of progress variation and the rate of real improvement.

- Finally, it makes it easier to shift goals during the change progress as new things about the organization are learned. This is hard to do when the perception is that the organization can go from its starting point to the future state in a straight, uninterrupted line. Change simply doesn't happen this way and the S-Curves help to make that visible.

Another way to think about S-Curves is the concept of *dynamic capabilities* introduced to me by Professor Mohan Tatikonda. Deployment of Six Sigma at Cummins is an example of a *dynamic capability* because it was purposefully built to continuously adapt to new needs and opportunities, rather than continuing to do the same thing it always did. In contrast, a *static* capability is pretty ordinary; many companies have this capability or if they don't have it, they can acquire and ramp it up pretty quickly. These ordinary, static capabilities don't provide enduring competitive advantage. But dynamic capabilities, because they specifically build on and are embedded in a company's own special history and culture, are inherently unique to that company. That is what makes them difficult, if not impossible, for competitors to acquire, adopt, or imitate. With a dynamic capability, your company is further along the S-Curves relative to its competitors. Still, the company must keep or increase pace to stay ahead of the competition. A way to think about the S-Curves is that an organization is putting in place dynamic capabilities that not only add value today but increase in value down the road because they adapt, improve and grow, and at a rate faster than the competitors.

I have found that a well-constructed set of S-Curves sets the foundation for change. It helps simplify a complex subject and makes it easier for people to understand what they must do and why as they provide support to a major change effort.

8

Communication and Education Planning

Once all of the change basics have been determined, it's time to develop a communication plan for getting the word out. A communication plan is important for achieving a return on the investment made to implement the change. It is not enough to hold a few senior executive leadership meetings and then send out some companywide e-mails or have a one-time, all-employee meeting and expect the change to happen. Successful change requires appropriately-timed, broad, and consistent communication so that everybody understands where the organization is going and their personal role in the change effort. Communication is a cascade beginning with senior executive leadership and progressing through the organization.

The strategy for communication that we applied when implementing Six Sigma, and one that I have applied successfully to other changes, is a "do and tell" versus a "tell and do" approach. The basic idea is to begin doing the work of putting the change into practice and measuring the results before communicating the change broadly to the larger organization. That way, when communication begins, it focuses on success and how that success is going to be multiplied. I have found that this approach beats the "tell and do" approach, which depends on success sometime in the future. It builds change communication on a foundation of success as opposed to a future promise and is more believable for the people of the organization.

The communication cascade begins with the senior executive leadership. The communication plan to the leadership team includes the following:

- Reasons for the change (the current state)

- Changes to be made

- Impact and value of the change

- The way the organization will look once the change is complete (the future state)
- The senior executive leader responsible for the effectiveness of the change
- People affected by the change
- Responsibilities of the people affected by the change
- The date the change effort will begin with milestones to achieve along the way
- Length of time the change is expected to take
- Training and education available for making the change
- The organization's processes that are expected to change
- Methods used to measure the change
- Resources required for the change (time, money and people)

Before the communication to the broader organization begins, basics of the communication plan include:

- What is the goal of each message?
- Why are we communicating?
- What messages do we want to send?
- What successes have we seen so far?
- Who will write the message?
- Who will own and deliver the message?
- How many times will each message be communicated?
- How often will we communicate each message?
- What will be communicated in each message?
- To whom will each message be communicated?
- How will each message be communicated (e-mail, presentation, video, and so on)?
- What languages will be used for communication? How and when will translation occur? Who is responsible for ensuring proper translation occurs?
- When will we communicate?
- How will we measure the effectiveness of each message?

INEFFECTIVENESS OF THE "TELL AND DO" APPROACH

Whenever possible I recommend following the "do and tell" approach. There are a couple of reasons why the "tell and do" approach is ineffective:

- The effect of the change is often overestimated and the time required is often underestimated. Communicating too early sets up expectations throughout the organization that cannot be met, causing cynicism towards this and future change efforts.

- Those who don't like the change have ammunition to use when things don't happen exactly the way they were described in the initial communication.

- Typically, the end-state of the change is uncertain because the future is unknown. This uncertainty is reduced with time as the change occurs within the cultural structure of the organization (see the S-Curves description). A change that works one way in one organization will be different in the next. It's hard to know what that difference will be until the process is started and has matured. One purpose of S-Curves and the future state is to recognize this reality and allow for adjustment with time and knowledge. This reality affects the communication by helping to keep it tuned to progress as it is made.

SUPPORTING THE "DO AND TELL" APPROACH

If change is to occur, the organization's leadership determines how people will learn about the change and their personal responsibilities. A traditional approach is to hire a consultant or develop a training package in-house, schedule classes, and "roll out" the training.

My experience is that it is very difficult to make this approach successful. The evidence for this can be seen in the graveyard of three-ring binders found on the shelves of many managers or in the organization's library or archive. These binders are the only remaining evidence of organization-wide training roll-outs that came and went.

As discussed earlier, hiring a consultant is a logical way to get change started, but it rarely works if the change process stops there. In most organizations, it is easy to ignore dictates from headquarters that are not expected to survive the test of time. This is especially the case when leaders don't spend their management capital reinforcing the behavior changes that are expected from the training, turning the responsibility over to one department or another. This leads to a fairly common reaction among many long-term employees who have seen this approach before.

They know that headquarters can't keep up the effort, and so they just wait for this most recent leadership brainstorm to pass.

How will people and processes behave differently as a result of the change (the future state)? Effective training and education describes the expected behavior, provides new tools and processes, and establishes the reinforcement mechanism. Further, it results in the application and practice of the required behavior. Application of project-centric, action-based training is the most effective way to use training in support of organizational change.

I don't intend to go through a detailed discussion of training design—that's for others to do. I have found that most discussions of what makes good training miss the mark by focusing too much on the training design and leaving out the most critical parts such as what change is expected, how people will be held accountable, and how change effectiveness is measured. Change becomes a training department effort, not a leadership effort.

The following discussion is an approach that I have actually seen work. It is not the only option, but I believe that it forms a template that can be copied.

The most successful change effort that I have experienced in a non-military setting is an implementation of Six Sigma. Success had little to do with the quality of the training material, which was generally consistent with other available packages. Rather, success was built on a set of principles that are transferrable to other efforts. The following discusses these principles.

Develop Clear Expectations, Requirements, and a Timeframe

The Six Sigma consultant initiated the most effective consulting contract I have ever experienced. What made it effective was that they said what they would do, they told us what we should do, and they made it clear that they would depart the organization at the end of two years, leaving us to own and to sustain the change effort. Because of the success of this approach, whether using a consultant or internal resources, I recommend that a firm end date be the starting point for contract negotiations or assignments.

Project-centered Training

Most working adults have not been in an academic setting for many years. They are no longer in the habit of studying, listening to lectures, or taking notes and tests. They need to learn practical lessons and apply what's been learned to their real work. Project-centered training is meant to meet this need.

In Six Sigma, the project is a problem to solve. For other change efforts, it is something else. The key is to define the project that will be used to reinforce any training and education, and require a project for all participants. A project problem could be a problem to solve, an assessment or audit, a plan to develop, a team engagement to accomplish a goal, or a redesign to implement. The project accompanies and supports any training and education received.

Measurable Results

Each person is responsible for a measurable outcome after receiving training and education. The result is tied to the project and can be measured in many different ways. A few examples include money, time, defects, or output. The purpose of the result is to give the project meaning and create accountability for the investment in education and training. Leadership would never invest money in a production line if it were not expected to produce value in excess of the investment. Training and education can be thought of in the same way. The return on investing for training and education begins with the project completed during training. Six Sigma tends to focus on cost savings that can be measured. As the process matures in the organization, the measures of success broaden but return on investment is always a useful success measure.

Buy Versus Create the Knowledge

Many organizations develop and support training and education internally. One of the few times this makes sense is when the organization's knowledge is so proprietary and unique that nobody else has the knowledge and it is a competitive advantage to keep the information in-house.

Generally, developing training internally is a mistake. Training departments tend to be seen as expendable, especially in businesses, and during difficult financial times are often one of the first groups to experience significant layoffs. Additionally, the investment required to maintain training material over time is significant. These investments include the following:

- The cost of hiring people to staff the training department
- The cost of creating training material
- The cost of translating material
- The cost of printing material
- The cost of shipping material

- The cost of changing and updating material in multiple languages
- The cost of supporting equipment
- The cost of maintaining material inventories
- The cost of making training material available globally
- The cost of staying current with the evolution of the discipline that the training addresses
- The cost of downsizing when difficult economic times come (which they always do!)

Furthermore, the time it takes to develop and launch effective training and education programs is significant. This often tests the leader's patience and, worse, can exceed the leadership's ability to remember why the training and education was needed in the first place. So the window of opportunity closes and the organization misses the chance to improve.

Generally, the knowledge necessary to develop a training program is relatively common and well understood as a discipline across the industry. Therefore, instead of developing training and education inhouse, contract with an external source whose training is consistent with the organization's future state and purchase as much of the process as possible.

There are several advantages to this approach. The dominant advantage is the ability to rapidly scale up and down when conditions affecting the organization change. Next, most credible consultants will tailor elements of the training material for your business. Finally, the most important advantage is that it allows the organization to move quickly once the decision that training and education are necessary to support a desired change is made.

So, buy it—don't create it.

(One note of caution: make sure the contract with the consultant is clear and concise and meets the needs of the organization. Don't allow the consultant to lock your organization into conditions that go beyond your needs and expectations. This effort requires leadership engagement and contract expertise.)

Connect the Education Plan and Communication Plan to Support a Do Then Tell Approach

The communication plan supports the education plan by informing people in the organization about the expectations for the training and education, the process, and the timing. The communication plan also clearly describes how education and training success is measured. The format for a communication plan was discussed earlier.

Establish a Support Infrastructure

Basically, there are three options an organization can use to support the training and education needed to implement change.

- Externally supported
- Internally supported
- Internal/external hybrid support

Option 1: Externally supported—contract with a consulting company to design and deliver all training and education. The main advantages of this approach are that it is easy to scale up and down with resource availability and subject-matter experts own the creation and delivery of the information shortening the development and validation time.

The main disadvantages are that it is easy to stop spending, but hard to restart. Also, people in the organization often don't feel responsible for the information. This makes establishment of accountability more difficult.

Option 2: Internally supported—establish an internal group responsible for development and delivery of training and education. The main advantages are that the people in the group are part of the organization and therefore understand how things work and can use real examples and experiences familiar to others. Because the information belongs to the organization, it is easier to control the message and how it is delivered. The people responsible for training are directly accountable to the organization's leadership.

The main disadvantage is the cost of sustaining the effort through economic cycles. Often, as said earlier, training and development departments are the first casualties of downsizing. Leadership may intend to bring the training department back when things are better, but the reality is that it is very hard to sustain previous efforts. Bringing the department back rarely happens effectively, and so all momentum is lost. A second disadvantage in the global organization is the ability to keep information up to date in all the languages needed. Maintenance and translation is very expensive and difficult to manage and sustain through time.

Option 3: An internal/external hybrid—responsibility is shared between a contracted consultant and internal resources. This collaboration can take many forms based on the needs of the organization. The main advantages are the ability to scale up and down quickly with economic conditions and the fact that the organization retains ownership of the information while using the external source for development, coordination, and delivery. However, management of the relationship can be difficult. It requires the merging of two organizational cultures into a mutually beneficial partnership where organizational goals, language, and processes are different. Therefore, careful selection of the partner is a precursor to success of the hybrid approach. This was the approach successfully applied to the Six Sigma implementation.

Each approach can work when managed well. Selection of the approach is based on the nature of the information and how it will be used. Some selection criteria include the following:

- Uniqueness of the information. Is the information and the intellectual property of the organization generally known and used broadly?

- Languages required. Will a single language be enough or are multiple languages necessary?

- Timeframe. How fast does the target audience need the information to begin the change process?

- Scope. Is it a requirement for everybody in the organization or just for a smaller subset?

- Resources required and committed. Are the necessary resources available and assigned?

- Longevity. Is there a time boundary?

Set Targets and Measure Performance

Define how progress will be measured using tangible metrics. Cost savings, delivery improvement, and quality upgrades are all tangible organizational metrics. Make it clear that targets will be set, progress tracked, and performance evaluated. Holding people accountable for making the changes defined by the training and education through tracking and evaluating performance is a key to successful complex organization change.

This approach is also applied to the consultant contract if consultants are part of the change. In our Six Sigma contract, we built in monetary incentives based on measurable cost savings resulting from the projects. The money available was significant and it helped keep the consulting group focused. The contract should also include penalty clauses if agreed goals are not met.

Communication and education planning are key elements to an overall change effort. It is important to apply the necessary effort to ensure that they are well thought out in support of the change. Don't allow them to become an afterthought belonging to someone other than leadership.

9

The Organization
Is a Living Thing

We talk about organizations in many different ways: culture, rhythms, personality, and maturity. These are terms used to describe living things. An organization, then, is a living thing. Like all living things, an organization has to grow and change or it decays and dies. Unlike living things, however, there is no assured final death or "last round-up" for the organization. The organization does not have to grow old and wither away. It can renew, regroup, recharge, and go on. Nation states are an example of organizations that continue on, changing dramatically over time. Today, the United States military looks nothing like it did 220 years ago. On the company front, P&G, GE, Cummins, and IBM have proven to be resilient. All these companies have shown the ability to change and grow, and therefore, survive. Since this book is about how to make organizational change, the *why* of making change is to, quite simply, prosper, survive, and thrive.

In a conference that I attended several years ago, I heard Gary Hamel talk about the "three generations of management." This concept has stayed with me and has been a useful idea when thinking about organizational change.

The first generation of management is the creator generation. The creator generation gives birth to the organization. It is their idea. This generation is responsible for everything that the organization is. The purpose, the people, and the products of the organization are all the "children" of the creator generation. These are the people who feel the greatest personal connection to the organization, treating it with all the love and affection that comes with that connection to creation.

The second generation of management is the maintainer generation. The creator generation is typically still around and has personal relationships with the maintainer generation. But, the creators are no longer involved in any of the day-to-day decisions or in the life of the organization. The maintainers try to maintain what the creator generation built. Their main role is to not screw it up. They tend to make fewer substantial changes. The maintainer generation keeps many of the old structures and attempts to live off past successes in the desire to keep them going. However, this can also mean losing sight of changing dynamics in the surrounding environment, leading to eventual difficulties and potential collapse.

The slide rule manufacturer, Pickett, is a favorite example. There was nothing wrong with the slide rule. I received one as a present after high school when I was bound for West Point and lots of math. But overnight, the slide rule became useless as handheld calculators became affordable and orders of magnitude more useful. Slide rule production ceased globally by the late 1970s and another company absorbed Pickett after 42 years of successful business. Pickett never saw it coming. (A history of the slide rule can be found here: http://sliderulemuseum.com/SR_Dates.htm.) Their fate is shared by many organizations.

The third generation of management is the pivotal generation. This generation has no direct connection to the creator generation. They might hear stories about them, and they know that the organization exists because of them. There might even be pictures of them scattered about the organization, but there is no personal attachment. The creators are a historical artifact with little to say to the pivotal generation about the current state of the organization. The pivotal generation presides over either the rebirth of the organization through change and growth, or it sees the break-up and death of the organization since it is no longer relevant in the current environment.

Knowing this generational pattern, the current leadership can assess the current state of the organization. Where is it along this generational continuum? By understanding its position, the leadership of the organization can plan an appropriate change response that will strengthen and prepare the organization for a new level of performance. S-Curves (discussed earlier) are a good mechanism for thinking about this kind of change effort.

THE KANO MODEL

The Kano Model (Figure 9.1) is a useful tool for helping leaders to think about what an organization might become. Noriaki Kano developed this model in the 1980s. The model is a thoughtful way to classify customer quality expectations. The quality expectation classifications are Basic, Performance, and Excitement. The Kano Model helps an organization to classify and understand the quality expectations of its customers, but is broadly applicable across a range of potential organization requirements. Examples include customer, product and service offerings, quality, change, or leadership requirements. Generally, it is a helpful model for thinking through a range of improvements to understand their effect.

The Kano Model

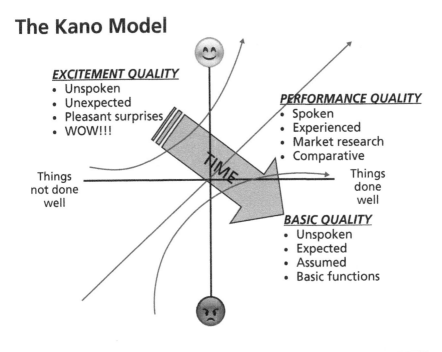

EXCITEMENT QUALITY
- Unspoken
- Unexpected
- Pleasant surprises
- WOW!!!

PERFORMANCE QUALITY
- Spoken
- Experienced
- Market research
- Comparative

Things not done well

Things done well

BASIC QUALITY
- Unspoken
- Expected
- Assumed
- Basic functions

Figure 9.1 The Kano Model is a useful tool for organizations looking toward change.

There are three classes of requirements:

- Basic
- Performance
- Excitement

Basic. Basic requirements are expected and unspoken. When talking to people about what they need or expect, basic requirements are rarely if ever discussed. For example, when shopping for a car, the buyer rarely discusses whether the windshield wipers or the door handles work, or if the wheels are round. These are simply unspoken expectations. Basic requirements, being unspoken expectations, go unnoticed if the requirement is met, even if met well. However, since it is an unspoken expectation, if not done well, failure very quickly causes a high degree of dissatisfaction. Basic requirements can be thought of as the ticket of entry. If these things are not done well, the organization is unlikely to survive for very long.

Performance. Performance requirements are spoken and come out of people's experiences. Performance requirements are comparative. If one organization is capable of meeting the requirement better than another organization, people will tend to go to the one that better meets the requirement. Performance requirements are the things people request. Examples include better fuel economy, use of higher-grade materials at a certain price, or provision of particular services. Performance requirements tend to be what people see and want, and what they are willing to pay for or use based on experience with other organizations or products. Generally, "more is better" relative to performance requirements and customer satisfaction is correlated to this performance. Since performance requirements are spoken and comparative, the organization that falls short in that regard with comparison to other organizations loses customers, users, or clients.

Excitement. Excitement requirements are like basic requirements in that they are unspoken. However, unlike basic requirements, excitement requirements are unexpected. Generally, they lie outside of people's experiences; therefore, people have no context for talking about them and can't express them as requirements. Many people can't remember life before the Internet, but at the time of its introduction, it was impossible to conceive of what it might do. People had no idea how to think about or express requirements related to the Internet. The computer on which I am typing this book can be seen through the same lens. In the early days of the computer, it was thought that the only people who might use computers were scientists. It was believed that the average person would *NEVER* have a need for something so exotic. Today, we carry more computing power in our pockets on our smart phones than was available to the known universe in the 1950s. There is simply no basis of comparison. Every day, new uses for computers are discovered and applications delivered that people don't expect or request.

An organization brings its skills and knowledge to a particular situation. It uses these skills and knowledge to identify new requirements that users can't see or define for themselves. Meeting excitement requirements makes an organization unique and distances it from other similar organizations. Delivering on excitement requirements is one of the dimensions that define an organization as world-class. This is also a mechanism for allowing the organization to grow and change.

A unique feature of meeting excitement requirements is it doesn't even have to be done all that well (at first) to improve satisfaction and not doing it at all has no impact because people don't expect it anyway. However, there is a natural and swift progression to excitement requirements. Today's excitement feature quickly becomes tomorrow's performance requirement and, in almost no time, becomes a basic requirement of any organization in the arena. An easy example is computer screens. In just a few short years, computer screens went from a black screen with a blinking green cursor to color with a GUI interface. Today, lacking color and this interface, a personal computer is unsalable and, with the advent of personal handheld devices, may yet become completely obsolete.

Using the Kano Model, an organization can evaluate its offerings in the following way:

- For each organization offering, decide on its classification. What features are basic, performance, or excitement?

- How well is the organization meeting basic requirements? Is the organization receiving any complaints about basic or expected offerings?

- How well does the organization's performance requirements measure up to those of other similar organizations or competitors? How do you know? How often do you investigate the answer to this question?

- How many offerings fit the excitement category? When was the last time an excitement-level offering was introduced? What work is underway to introduce an excitement-level product or service? If the excitement bucket is empty, your organization might be approaching a critical time in its ability to continue. This is a good indicator that the organization may have lost sight of its environment and is becoming a potential candidate for an upcoming struggle.

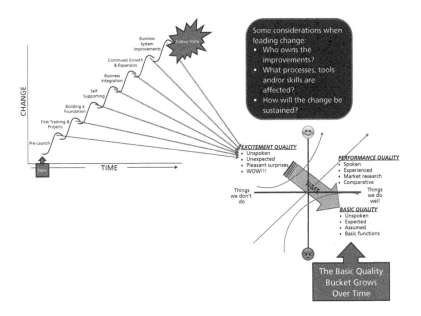

Figure 9.2 The combination of the Kano Model with S-Curves allows an organization to see where it is going and classify changes.

Combining the Kano Model with S-Curves (Fig. 9.2) creates a powerful set of tools for thinking about where the organization is going and how to classify changes being undertaken as the organization makes its way along the S-Curves to the future state. As an organization moves up the S-Curves toward the future state, its offerings pass from excitement to performance to basic.

Whatever is new to the organization meets an excitement-level requirement. That new capability or product moves quickly to a basic-level requirement, unspoken and expected. Each new S-Curve begins as an excitement feature that ultimately moved to basic. This pattern is repeated as long as the organization is growing and changing and the basic bucket of requirements to maintain grows. A key question is how will the organization effectively manage the increasing requirements of the basic bucket of requirements.

THE EFFECT OF CULTURE

Culture is the personality of the organization. Culture is made up of many elements. Some of these elements include the following:

- Whether the main source of leadership selections is internal or external

- Whether the products delivered by the organization are durable goods, consumer goods, marketable services, public services, private services, charitable services, or something else

- Whether the decision making process is top down or consensus

- Whether the organizational span is local, domestic, regional or global

- Whether the organizational speed is fast or slow

- Whether the environment is competitive or collegial

- Whether the organization is public or private

- Whether the employee profile is college, high school, or indeterminate

The culture is greatly influenced by the organization's leader. Given time, the leader's personality will be reflected in the culture of the organization. How much of the leader's personality comes through into the organization is also a function of whether leaders come from inside or outside the organization. This aspect of culture certainly doesn't happen quickly, but it does happen.

Knowing the culture of the organization provides clues about how to make changes. Each of the elements above, plus others, either enable desired changes or create barriers to desired changes. For example, if an organization is consensus-based, it is hopeless to drive change using a top-down approach. Making a decision behind closed doors in the CEO's office and then announcing it to the organization without building the necessary consensus is doomed in a consensus-based culture. The organization will act like a mass of gelatin, absorbing the directions one after the other until senior executive leadership either gets tired or bored of the effort. Senior executive leadership will then either declare victory or allow the change to melt away. An organization is much stronger than any individual leader. Not knowing the culture makes all change difficult, if not impossible.

A much higher potential for success comes to those who use the existing culture to create and sustain change over time.

The military is one of the best examples of an organization that is very accepting of a top-down approach to decisions. There is freedom of action, but it is freedom of action within the confines of the decision that is handed down through the ranks. A charitable organization may be on the other end of the spectrum from the military. With leaders, a board, donors, volunteers, and those being served, there are often many voices who expect to be heard during the decision-making process. People in the organization have been conditioned to expect that they will participate in the decision-making. Therefore, they will rebel, both passively and actively, against a decision for which they have no ownership.

Most organizations tend to fall somewhere between these two boundaries. Knowing how the organization operates allows the plan of action for both making and implementing decisions to be successful. These cultural elements impact how the organization operates. Assessing decisions and actions in light of these cultural elements is an aid to implementation. Ignoring the corporate culture ensures barriers will arise to frustrate the implementation of the organization's plans and actions.

As a living entity, the organization has a personality and feelings that are defined within its culture. Paying attention to the culture improves the chances for successful change.

10

Change Takes Time

I have developed a simple equation for helping leadership understand and plan how much time a focused change can take. The larger the organization, the more time it will take. This seems obvious. However, I have watched very intelligent, thoughtful people drastically underestimate the time it takes to make a successful organization-wide change. This simple rule-of-thumb is shown here (Figure 10.1). If it takes five eight-hour days to make a change in an organization of 100 people, then given a known number of people, it is easy to calculate how many eight-hour days it will take to implement a change. I assume a well-run

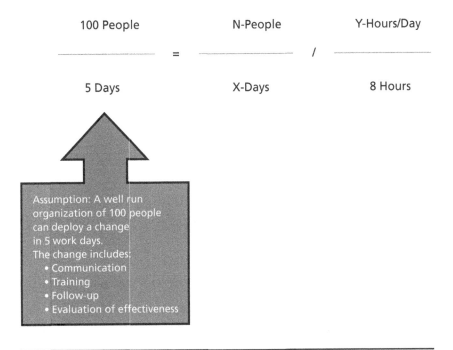

$$\frac{100\ People}{5\ Days} = \frac{N\text{-}People}{X\text{-}Days}\ /\ \frac{Y\text{-}Hours/Day}{8\ Hours}$$

Assumption: A well run
organization of 100 people
can deploy a change
in 5 work days.
The change includes:
 • Communication
 • Training
 • Follow-up
 • Evaluation of effectiveness

Figure 10.1 Time guideline for making change.

organization with 100 people could implement a change over a 40-hour week if they did nothing else. This equation is only a guideline and is really intended to get leadership thinking seriously about the real time commitment required. It is not intended to be nor is it a statistically valid formula. Given the number of variables that will impact the change effort, precision is impossible anyway. So, I encourage the reader to use it in the spirit it was intended—as a simple guideline that can help leaders plan for the time it takes to implement change.

THE SEVEN MANAGEMENT PLANNING TOOLS

Following the decision to make a change, the change effort requires planning and organization. The Seven Management Planning Tools (referenced earlier) were created for just this task. The value of the Seven Management Planning Tools is the linking of tools and processes together for the purpose of creating a plan that can be followed over time. One important outcome of this cross-functional process is that it helps leadership see the amount of work required to successfully implement a desired change. The time and work required is *always* more than leadership anticipates. The Planning Tools provide an organized approach to seeing this reality. I am not going to explain the tools here as there is a lot of material available describing them. The seven tools are:

1. Affinity diagram
2. Interrelationship diagraph
3. Tree diagram
4. Prioritization matrix
5. Matrix diagram
6. PDPC chart (Process Decision Program Chart)
7. Activity network diagram

Using the Seven Management Planning Tools is not the only effective planning approach. It is, however, one that I have used and found to be effective and is a good complement to the S-Curves for planning growth and maturity.

FMEA (FAILURE MODES AND EFFECTS ANALYSIS)

A step often lacking in most change efforts is an analysis of what can go wrong. Fail-safes need to be developed to prevent failures. (A simple definition of a fail-safe is a mechanism that prevents unconscious errors. An example is a mandatory field on a computerized form.) Mitigation/reaction plans that address failures that cannot be prevented, only

CHANGE:							
A	B	C	D	E	F	G	H
ELEMENTS OF THE CHANGE	HOW CAN THE ELEMENT FAIL?	WHAT IS THE IMPACT OF THE FAILURE?	SCORE THE IMPACT (1-LOW TO 10-HIGH)	HOW LIKELY IS THAT THE FAILURE WILL OCCUR? (1-LOW TO 10-HIGH)	HOW EFFECTIVE IS YOUR ABILITY TO DETECT THE FAILURE? (1-LOW TO 10-HIGH)	MULTIPLY COL DxExF SORT FROM LARGEST TO SMALLEST RESULT	WHAT ACTIONS ARE NEEDED TO PREVENT OR REACT TO THE FAILURE?

Figure 10.2 The failure modes and effects analysis (FMEA) modified for making a change.

reacted to when they happen, also need to be developed. The failure modes and effects analysis (FMEA) was originally designed to help understand what could go wrong with automotive parts and products. It is a mistake, however, to see this approach applicable only to automobile manufacturing. An FMEA can also be used to understand what can go wrong with processes and plans. The FMEA helps to identify unintended consequences that can cause plans to go awry or problems that develop during and following plan implementation.

This is important because when planning a change, I have found that planners tend to look only at the positives and rarely anticipate or talk about anything negative occurring. This is only natural since a person or group works hard to persuade an organization to do something different based on the good things that will happen. This is called marketing. To admit that there might be some negatives creates doubt that this is a good change and gives ammunition to those who are resistant to the change. When making change, it is prudent to conduct an FMEA not only on the plan but also on the change itself. I have included a basic format in Figure 10.2 that can be applied to any change initiative, although, it is important to tailor it to meet individual situations.

Once the analysis of potential failures is completed, resolutions for the most important and likely failures are developed prior to the start of the change effort.

SMALL EXPERIMENTS

In a complex organization, it is difficult to implement broad scale change all at once. A better strategy is to consider a number of small experiments. These experiments are conducted to test the change before the whole organization is committed to it.

A place to begin the change with a small experiment is with a group that recognizes the need for the change and wants to be early adopters. This makes a good test bed for the change because early adopters understand that the change process won't be perfect and are willing to accept a lack of perfection in return for being first. This is a group that wants to see the change succeed, often because they need it, and they will help fix the problems to make it better. They also tend to recognize that participation gives them a say in the final outcome and for this reason they are motivated to help.

Beginning with small experiments enables growth and maturity of the change itself. It is rare that a change performs exactly as expected during first implementation, even with the best potential failure analysis. Small experiments make it possible to make changes with early adopters, so the whole organization is spared the improvement process that can sometimes be substantial.

Adapting the schedule of change to individual sub-unit maturity is also important for making a successful change. There is a need to allow for variation in the rate and pace of implementation of the change because every part of the organization doesn't need the same improvement at the same time.

This is one of the main ideas of S-Curve thinking. In a complex organization, individual sub-units may have already adopted certain elements of the change through their normal leadership improvement processes and be far along in its maturity. The key is to recognize these differences and drive movement in a common direction towards the future state. Planned improvements are keyed to the needs and maturity of the sub-unit.

The only given regarding a change is that the whole organization is going to change. The change has been defined and the organization will progress toward it with the caveat that the change will likely be modified as the organization matures and learns. The specific changes made at a specific time are consistent with the needs and maturity of the sub-units. It is also very important that progress is reviewed and monitored by leadership.

11

The Importance of a Common Language

All organizations have various forms of internal and external boundaries. An example of an external boundary is the one that exists between the organization and a customer or a supplier. The supplier and the customer are different organizations, which creates a boundary. An internal boundary might exist between departments or functions in an organization. Boundaries are not good or bad; they just are.

Functional, physical, and measurement boundaries are common regardless of the size of an organization. A global organization is significantly affected by its ability to communicate effectively and efficiently across its boundaries. And there are many boundaries to consider. Possible boundaries include the following:

- Physical locations
- Subordinate units
- Functions
- Layers of leadership
- Languages and dialects
- Education levels
- Distance
- Products and services produced and offered
- Absorbed organizations, purchased or merged
- Regional culture
- Work ethic and traditions

Each boundary presents a different set of challenges when making change. An important strategy that will reduce some of this complexity is the adoption of a common organizational language. A common language makes it easier to talk together and, therefore, easier to work together when implementing large-scale change.

DEVELOPING A COMMON LANGUAGE

A common language is a set of terms, standards, definitions, measures, processes and expectations that are the same no matter where one looks in the organization. A common language is not for every little thing that the organization does. It applies to those aspects of the organization that make it unique, are critical to customers, and key to organizational results. There are several reasons why it is important to develop a common language in an organization.

It is very easy for people in organizations to feel lost and to forget that they belong to something much larger than themselves. A common language helps people see where they fit in the broader context of the organization. It also helps people feel that they are part of the larger whole by possessing special knowledge that is unique to their organization. This *specialness* and feeling of belonging helps motivate people to want what is best for the organization and its customers. A simple example of this idea of specialness and the feeling of belonging is wearing a common uniform. Most who wear it feel a sense of belonging to something larger than themselves.

W. Edwards Deming, the famous quality guru, spoke of the importance of operational definitions for organizations. If terms are not commonly defined, it is impossible for people to communicate and work together. The words that they use must mean the same thing if actions taken are to be useful to the product or service delivered. Think of the importance of having agreement on the measurement system to use. If one part of the organization uses metric and the other uses US Customary, nothing that they make will work together. And this is just one simple example! This is also true of organizational measures. If the measures aren't commonly defined, it is impossible to accurately assess how the organization is performing. For example, if inventory on hand is measured differently across the organization, it is impossible to know how much inventory actually exists.

The terms, processes, and expectations of the organization are the focus when creating a common language. What is the common work of the organization? How is it organized? What are the key words to be used? These are all conscious decisions that the leadership of the organization is responsible to make, to broadly communicate, and to ensure consistency of use throughout the organization.

Sports provide a good analogy here. In American football, each team has a language all its own. The language that is developed is important because it tells each player what to do during each individual play of the game. Without the common language, players would run around doing what they thought was best. The resulting outcome would be chaos. It is the same in any organization.

A common language facilitates working effectively together across boundaries. By focusing on the products and services of the organization, a common organizational language is developed that helps build understanding regarding direction and priorities.

Imagine what it would be like if there were no common language for discussing the work of the organization. Each term and word used would need to be defined and clarified. This would not only be frustrating but, also, very inefficient.

Six Sigma is an example of a common language at many companies. The common processes and tools apply to and can be used to improve all organizational activities. A second example is a business operating system (BOS). Companies use a BOS to standardize functional processes, definitions, and roles globally. The business operating system is the framework for continuous improvement of the processes, tools, and skills needed to deliver products and services to customers and to eliminate waste and variation across a complex company. The common language established by the BOS enhances communication across the many organizational boundaries that exist.

A third example is the United States Army. The functions are the various branches: armor, infantry, artillery, and so on. Each branch has a school that defines the language and that language is coordinated with the other branches so that communication is possible both within each branch and across the branches. Each school educates its members on the language that governs its operations. This is important because there is implicit danger in Army activities and it's important that people do the work the right way every time because failure can have catastrophic consequences. The point here is that a common organizational language gives people the ability to work together in complex organizations.

The most important step in creating a common language is developing a framework that provides the structure and context for the work. This framework answers the question, "What does this organization do and how does it do it?" The answer lies between micro-level process mapping describing individual activities and macro-level strategic business modeling. The framework describes how the organization goes to market or provides its services. The purpose of the organizational framework is to create a model showing how micro-level processes fit together and the organizational activity needed to accomplish its macro-level strategies.

The organization strategy and the organization model are both used to develop the framework. What business or service are we in? What products or services do we provide? What do we stand for? What is our approach to making our products and services available? This is all information for creating the framework. The framework uses this information to describe what an organization has to do to delight customers and stakeholders, deliver business commitments, meet organizational health needs, and delight its people. This isn't meant to be a future-oriented process. It is a description of the reality of the work done to deliver an organization's products and services.

DEFINING BIG PROCESS ELEMENTS

The next step in developing the BOS framwork is to define the big process elements of the organization. The questions (the Baldrige National Quality Award is an excellent model for a complete set of questions) to answer include:

- How do customers find out about our products and services?
- How do we determine customer needs, requirements, and expectations?
- How do we decide what products and services to provide?
- How do we develop new and innovative products and services?
- How do we make our products and services available to our customers?
- How do we produce our products and services?
- How do we maintain our products and services?
- How do we ensure our employees' needs, requirements, and expectations are met?
- How do we ensure compliance with relevant financial laws and rules?
- How do we give people the information that they need to do their jobs?
- How do we use additional support capabilities to meet needs, requirements, and expectations, both internally and externally?
- How do we measure the success of our products and services?
- How do we measure the effectiveness of our critical processes?
- How do we measure the capability of our people to do the work of the organization?
- How do we measure customer loyalty and satisfaction?
- How do we measure the effectiveness of our leadership system?
- How do we measure the impact of our organization on the communities where we operate?

In the following paragraphs, I will describe a generic structure for the different elements of an organizational framework (Figure 11.1).

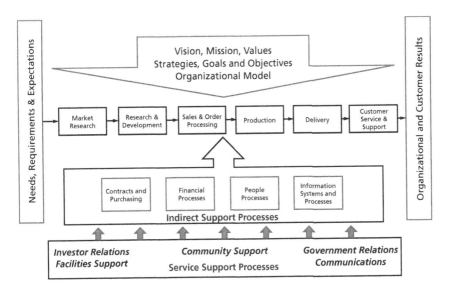

Figure 11.1 The different elements of the organizational framework.

Direct Customer and Business Support Processes

These are the processes that work together to deliver products and services to the organization's customers. These processes define the basics of how the organization accomplishes its mission. In business, the output of these processes is what customers pay for.

Indirect Support Processes

The processes that provide support to the direct support processes tend to be a combination of business/service and compliance related processes. Business/service related processes and support are things like financial tracking, employee services, information support systems, and so on. Compliance activities are the things that an organization must do to remain viable in its regulatory and legal environment. These are the requirements for entry into a country or market as well as the activities that are required by law and regulation. They include the activities that are necessary for the running of the organization, but are not in the direct chain of activities required to deliver the organization's products and services. These activities compete for a finite number of resources (people, time, and money). Identifying which activities are critical to customers and to the organization is important for Indirect Support Process effectiveness.

Service Support Processes

These are the processes that are needed to fulfill the very specific and targeted needs of the organization. Everyone in the organization uses outputs of the service support processes. These processes add little direct or indirect support to the products and services of the organization. They can be purchased. They are important to the overall health of the organization. These processes include activities such as security, facilities planning, investor relations, and communications. Different organizations will have different service support processes based on the kind of work that they do.

Once the framework has been established, the next task is to define the functions of the organization. Using the framework, identify the areas of capability needed to accomplish the purpose of the processes that have been outlined in the framework. Two obvious functional areas are finance and human resources. These functional areas are groupings of processes, methods, and capabilities that can be collected together because of their common subject matter and output. Together they form areas of expertise. It is important to establish ownership, accountability, and responsibility for these functional areas in the development of the common organizational language, driving improvement, and making changes. Each of the functional areas has a leader at the top level of the organization. This leader is accountable for the performance of the function's critical processes, methods, and capabilities. A critical activity is defined as an activity needed to support the purpose of the organization.

The following is a set of basic definitions for the three areas (processes, methods, and knowledge, skills and capabilities). Much has been written elsewhere on these subjects, so I will not attempt to cover them in detail. The point is that everything that happens in an organization falls into one of these three areas. Ensuring ownership and accountability for each area in a structured way is important for any organization.

- **Processes.** The set of coordinated and linked activities necessary for delivering the outputs of the organization. Each process is individually defined as a set of steps that, when connected together, will deliver products and services to customers and results for the organization.

- **Methods.** Used in the processes. Methods can be physical (that is, computers, hammers, machine tools, and so on). Methods can also be information based (that is, spreadsheets, forms, templates, and so on). Methods are used to make the processes work.

- **Knowledge, Skills and Capabilities.** Needed by people who use the tools to do the work of the processes. Knowledge, skills, and capabilities are connected to the critical processes and the tools required. A broad, general description of skills is inadequate. They must be connected to the processes of the organization and driven by the needs of customers and other stakeholders. Otherwise, the ability of the organization to meets its requirements is compromised.

A common organizational language is fundamental to the successful delivery of high quality products and services because it enables people to work effectively and efficiently together in ways that are impossible without it. Such a language underlies the ability of the organization as a whole and individuals to learn at a fast rate—faster than the competition—and so is essential to organizational growth and sustainability over time.

12

It's the Processes

E verything that the organization produces is the result of a process or processes. Literally everything happens through processes. Nothing that comes out of an organization is a spontaneous event created out of nothing. There is some input (for example, information, material, energy, requests, and so on). The input is then gathered and acted upon by people through a set of steps that produce an output that is used by the organization's customers or as inputs to other processes in the organization. This is the essence of a process.

The effectiveness of the organization's processes to deliver results that meet customer expectations contributes to an organization's success or failure. This is a very simple idea; however, it is an idea that is easily lost in a complex organization.

Many things crowd in on senior executive leadership and demand their attention. In the complex, multi-functional, global organization, the impact of the investment community, government rules and regulations, myriad customer issues, a diverse employee population and its needs, different cultural norms, and the need for leadership diversity all absorb leadership time and attention. Specific process effectiveness and improvement is often invisible to the senior executive leadership because they are insulated from it. This requires them to trust that lower levels of leadership in the organization are paying attention. However, for a number of reasons (internal politics, communication complexity, distance from organization leadership, and many others) attention from local leadership just doesn't happen. It is my firm belief that one of the central roles of leadership at all levels of an organization is to understand the organization's critical-to-customer processes and to ensure that clear ownership of those processes is established, that effectiveness as defined and measured by customers is visible, and that priority-based continuous improvement and standardization occurs wherever possible. Lacking this focus by leadership on process effectiveness, the products and services delivered to customers progressively fail to meet requirements. The organization becomes increasingly uncompetitive and eventually disappears from the scene once there are no customers for its products and services. Make no mistake, this level of focus is really hard to do. It is difficult, at least in part, because it requires taking the long view and can become tedious. But the payoff is substantial.

THE PROCESSES AROUND US

Processes are all around us. The following is a discussion of the different kinds of processes. It is intended to give you a way to begin thinking about the processes that ultimately affect an organization's customers.

Have you ever made a cake? Have you ever made a cake without following a recipe? Unless you are an accomplished chef, the answer is undoubtedly "No." Why? Without a recipe, the result is generally fit for the garbage. A recipe is a process. It is a step-by-step guide for making an edible cake. If a step is missed, the quality of the cake is affected. Making a cake is a simple process, but a process nonetheless.

Going to work every morning is a process. For most of us, the day begins with the blaring of an alarm of some sort. Waking up is followed by a series of events that tend to be the same each day, especially on a workday. Why do you set the alarm for a specific time? You know when to set the alarm because you know how long it takes to get ready and travel to work in order to arrive at the scheduled time. Preparing for work every morning is a repeatable process. Some people are more disciplined than others at preparing for work and they arrive every day at the same time; others arrive at various times and are even occasionally late. This phenomenon can be explained by realizing some processes are better designed and controlled than others.

Making a sale is a process. The starting point is a product offering and a potential customer. There are a series of steps that the sales person goes through to attract the interest of the customer and ultimately seal the deal. There is variation in how this is done depending on the sales person's skill to interpret the behavior of the potential customer. But there is a pattern that exists and the expert sales person knows how to use that pattern to the greatest advantage in order to make the sale.

Creating a product is a process. The process starts with a requirement or need. The designer responds to that requirement with potential product ideas until finally settling on an idea that is capable of meeting the need. The design is created as a prototype, tested, improved, tested again, and improved again. Great product companies include manufacturing, sales, purchasing, and service people (among other functions) in the design process to respond to the new design by preparing their functional areas for the new product. The product is then introduced for sale. Depending on the complexity of the product, this process is more or less detailed. But, it is a process and not following it leads to poor product performance for customers.

Executing the supply chain is a process. The supply chain is the end-to-end flow of information and material from its raw state to the customer for use and disposal. Planning, developing, sourcing, making, delivering, and servicing (these are the elements of the globally accepted Supply Chain Operational Reference Model) products for customers is the result of linking specific processes together so that customers receive what they have purchased. There are inputs to and outputs from each process. Understanding the effectiveness of each individual input and output is critical to the uninterrupted and flawless flow of information and material in the supply chain. It is fundamental to the quality experienced by the organization's customers.

Setting targeted, continuous improvement priorities is the work of leadership at all levels. The purpose of this difficult work is to provide customers with products and services that work as expected. The result of this flawless flow of information and material is quality in the eyes of the organization's customers. *There is no more important work for the organization.* The inability or unwillingness to do this often spells a short life for the organization as customers move on to products and services that work for them.

THE PROCESS NERD FEST

Before starting this section, I have a confession to make. I am a process nerd. As such it took me a long time to understand that simply documenting processes isn't valuable to an organization. I ran many process nerd fests. I want to lay out in this section how to make the documentation of processes meaningful and valuable.

A phenomenon that occurs in many organizations is the *process nerd fest*. A process nerd fest happens when the process people of an organization come together to understand an issue. The work very quickly turns from understanding what the issue is and what to do about it to a drive to document the organization's processes because the process people understand that the secret to the solution is in the processes. However, because they are process people, the documentation of the processes becomes the work instead of working on solving the issue.

Often, these process nerd fests become irrelevant because when limited progress is made on actually solving the issue, senior executive leadership loses faith. More importantly, the value of understanding the processes of the organization is lost because results of the work are hard to find. The term *process nerd fest* is not meant to be insulting. I have often played the role of giant process nerd and the failure rate of the work was high. This is a particularly insidious problem in larger organizations because there are simply more people around to do this kind of work. And, by the way, they want to do it really well. The whole thing just gets out of control.

The only way to avoid the process nerd fest is to focus on the real, measurable customer or business need. The sponsor of the work is a senior executive leader who has the most ownership for the success of the work and drives the team to a focused, meaningful, and measurable result on a schedule that has a clearly established end point. Lacking these things, it is almost a certainty that the team will wander off course into the land of the process nerd fest.

The interesting thing is that everybody is right when it comes to working on the processes that get in the way of success for the customer and for the business. I have read many books on the subject, gone to seminars, and learned from my own and others' work over the years. All the people writing and consulting and speaking are right, but they are also all wrong. Their perspectives tend to narrow as their focus shifts from figuring out how to get work done to selling their own ideas. This gets in the way of taking a more balanced view.

The Quality People Have It Right

Deming, Crosby, the Feigenbaums, Juran and many others through the years were right. Understanding processes, using data, statistical analysis, process control and capability, and process ownership is the language of continuous process improvement for better customer and business results. But for many people in leadership, it is analogous to speaking Latin in the 21st century. It makes no sense. And the people in quality seem incapable of consistently making what they have to say make sense to the people running businesses. The quality efforts of many organizations, while originally meant to improve product and service quality, turn into programs for the quality people to manage. Essentially, the quality people are told that they are supported—just don't bother leadership with it, "Go away and tell us when you are done." The quality people fail to turn the language of quality into the language of business: money, customers, products, and shareholders. This breakdown in communication impedes improvement because the business leadership doesn't see a direct relationship to the most important customer and organizational measures. The quality and business people are simply speaking different languages and can't understand each other.

The Business People Have It Right

Business schools teach people how to see the macro world of business. Profit and loss, business strategy, product differentiation, and share-holder value is the language of business leadership. These areas are the ultimate measures of organizational success and are, therefore, a critically important aspect of running the organization. In a small organization, these areas are an everyday reality. Small actions can have a huge effect on the success or failure of smaller organizations. In a larger, more complex organization, the numbers are so large and their reach so vast that the tendency is to focus on what can be collected and analyzed.

What can be most easily collected and analyzed is money. It is the rare senior executive leadership team that truly understands, in a way that affects priority setting and decision making, that the money is simply an end result of the underlying processes. They talk about the money; they plan for the use of the money; they count and measure the money; they look at ratios built on the money. It's all about the money. Don't misunderstand; the money is critical to organizational survival and needs to be measured. But thinking that the organization can be run only by measuring and managing the money is an illusion that has unintended consequences. There are many books that discuss subjects like balanced scorecards, Baldrige, and total quality that can be helpful. The reality is that money is the language of organizational leadership. Because leadership makes all of the critical decisions affecting the organization, if the quality people are speaking quality and the leadership is speaking money, there is an unintentional but inevitable communication breakdown. Eventually the leadership quits listening to the quality people altogether because what they are saying just sounds like noise.

The Consultants Have It Right

Often the consultants have something valuable to sell. But, as discussed earlier, they are in business to sell their services. They sell what they know. Often, their language is a combination of business and quality language, but is, by definition, limited to what they know and to models that define them. They speak their own organizational language that is different from the organization's language. This difference can be difficult to reconcile and often limits the potential good that the consulting interaction can do.

They Also Have It Wrong

So, while they have it right in their own way, they also have it wrong. It is really the merging of all of it. The quality people have to be seen as business people who have some great processes in order to improve results for the customers and the business. The business people have a responsibility to drive results in a balanced way, by establishing critical priorities, and driving teams to produce results that can be measured in a variety of ways, including money. The consultants bring specialized knowledge that can help an organization move forward if the leadership can be clear about how the consultants' knowledge fits with the organization's expectations, deliverables, and timeframes.

In the end, it is all connected to the organization's processes. Understanding the importance of processes gives the organization a level of control over its products and services that will ensure customer loyalty because those products and services are better than the competition's.

13

Looking Inside

Toyota popularized the idea that finding problems is a good and useful thing to do. Every problem found and solved made the company's products better for its customers and users. Unfortunately, in many organizations, problems are treated as an element of the internal competition for position and an indicator of poor leadership. Problems are reflected on the organization or individual's report card so it is difficult to make the problems visible. Therefore, problems are seen as a bad thing. The challenge for leadership is to create an environment that encourages and values problems found—the thornier and tougher the better. One of the keys to finding problems is a healthy, active, and responsive assessment culture.

AUDITING

The value of assessment has been ignored in much of the business and non-business world because of the mistaken assumption that assessment is the same as an audit. They are, however, very different.

Let's start with an audit. Auditing is checking to see if people are following policy, standards, regulations, and laws. An audit is fundamentally about compliance and does not test whether the organization is effective. In fact, auditing is generally unconcerned about the value of the organization's outputs to the users. The audit is focused on answering the question "Did you or did you not do something?" There is a basic assumption that if the organization passes the audit there will be a good result. Therefore, the audit tends to be a pass/fail system.

Compliance auditing didn't start out to be this. The idea was that there are best ways to do things. If the best way to do things could be codified into standards, organizations could be audited for compliance. Compliance would then extrapolate to a good product or service. This basically good idea found its way to the graveyard of all good ideas: bureaucracy. The standards were handed to agencies that were responsible for their stewardship. These agencies were staffed with people. These people weren't going to do this work for free, so the agency had to charge for its stewardship. As the standards were implemented more and more broadly, the size of the agencies grew. This required the agency to build self-sustaining business models with rules and governance that insured the continuance of the agencies themselves. The unfortunate result became a focus on keeping the agency viable and a loss of value to the organizations that they were intended to serve. This is a natural human phenomenon. It is a self-protection mechanism because real people are depending on these agencies for their livelihoods. We can't be surprised when the survival of the agency becomes the priority. But it has doomed compliance auditing to be something that organizations dread. The compliance audit, in many cases, has lost its ability to add real value to an organization beyond remaining "legal."

There is also the issue of audit personnel. Compliance auditing is not, generally, a career with a future in and of itself. Auditors tend to come in three varieties: people who use the audit as a mechanism to drive improvement, people fresh out of school, and people at the end of their careers (see the chapter on consultants).

The people who use the audit as a mechanism to drive improvement don't think of the audit as an end in itself, but a means to better organizational performance. They work with people in the organization to understand its culture, products, and services while balancing the established rules of the certifying agencies. These people can be very helpful for driving a continuous improvement approach to the audit process. However, I have seen them struggle to keep the rules and a desire to be helpful in balance, which creates a lot of stress for both themselves and the organizations they audit.

The people fresh out of school use their time as an auditor to learn about how organizations work. They are sent to audit organizations with which they have no experience. Their audit is based on checklists about which they understand little beyond the basics. About the time they do become competent, they have moved onto their real career in business, politics, law, or any of a number of other professions.

Then there are the more seasoned auditors. These are people who tend to be at the end of their careers. They bring a particular knowledge of their area of specialty and apply that to their practice of compliance auditing. However, they tend not to have comparable knowledge of how organizations actually work. On the positive side, the seasoned auditor can teach while auditing by sharing best practices seen other places. Too often, however, I have seen this type of auditor use their specialized knowledge to deliver "gotcha findings" that aren't helpful to the audited organization. The organization dreads the arrival of these people. So the audit becomes a game to give the auditors only what they need to see.

I originally saw this game played in the Army during the Annual General Inspection (AGI). The AGI was an audit of the unit's conformance to army rules and regulations. Does each soldier have the defined gear? Are the barracks being maintained to army standard? Does the unit have all of its authorized equipment? Are maintenance records maintained and documented to army standard? Anyway, you get the idea.

So what was the response of the unit? The commander couldn't have a failed AGI on his record. So, the unit began preparations two months in advance of the event. All paperwork was reviewed and mistakes corrected so that it would conform. The barracks were painted, furniture fixed, floors shined, and all other manner of preparations were made to the physical facilities. My favorite event, however, was maintenance shop preparation. The unit would pick its most disheveled soldier and its most broken down five-ton truck. The truck would be loaded with all of the spare parts that were outside of army standard, and then both truck and soldier would be sent to the range with a tent and enough rations for the duration of the AGI. This activity had nothing to do with the mission of the unit, yet it went on year after year, unit after unit. And, incredibly, everybody knew the game, including the AGI inspectors, because they had all been in units during the bulk of their careers and had done the same things! By the way, rarely did a unit fail the AGI.

Imagine my amazement when I saw exactly the same behavior in the business world as an organization prepared for its compliance audit. Paperwork was fixed, the facility cleaned, and certain people were asked to stay home with pay during the audit. Astonishing! None of these activities helped the business deliver better products and services to its customers, but typically resulted in a "passed" audit and the receipt of a framed, signed certificate verifying the quality of the organization's processes.

The problem with this approach and its result can be seen in the generally uncompetitive quality of many American cars through the last decades of the 20th century and early in the 21st century. All of the American car companies have flags flying and framed certificates in their lobbies verifying that they have passed the audits given by various agencies, but year in and year out the customer evaluation of their products generally fell well below that of the Japanese and Germans. The compliance audit has a place, but it has proven itself to be incapable of impacting the quality of products and services in a reliable way. The compliance audit consistently fails the test of helping organizations see its problems.

ASSESSMENT

There is a place for compliance audits. We need them to ensure that rules and laws are being followed, but I believe it is a mistake to see them as being capable of much more than that. Helping organizations see problems is the role of assessment. Assessments are a tool of leadership at all levels and are continuous in that they are going on throughout the year. Assessments are focused on the organization's processes and are used for the purpose of finding where things aren't working as they should, which results in problems for customers. They also serve to meet leadership's need to see, prioritize, and fix the organization's biggest problems in order to improve the quality of the products and services that the organization's customers receive.

Assessment can take many forms:

- A functional assessment is used to determine if the basics of the function are in place and operating in a way that supports the needs of the organization and its customers.

- A process assessment investigates specific processes to understand how the work of the organization is performed and its impact on results measures. It seeks to identify gaps and problems for continuous improvement work.

- A supply chain assessment seeks to understand how the flows of the organization are working. The focus is the connection between processes. Are the hand-offs between processes happening the way they should? Does information and material flow without waste and disruption from suppliers all the way to the organization's customers? Wherever a flow disruption is found, a potential exists for continuous improvement.

- Baldrige assessments allow the leadership of an organization to understand how well its leadership system is working. Is the organization designed to address all of the elements that define high-quality products and services for its customers?

- External assessors provide the leadership of an organization with an impartial, third-party view of improvement opportunities that are frequently invisible to those directly responsible for the work.

The common characteristic of all these assessments is that they address the leadership's need to understand the problems that exist in the organization. The cultural attitude that must exist for assessments to provide real value is a clearly expressed expectation that says "we want to see our problems." Assessments are not a report card of performance. An assessment framework is intended to reveal the areas where improvement is needed.

The assessment framework begins with a set of questions that provides a detailed and consistent review of how processes are functioning. These questions are designed to understand the following:

- How the organization's customers, their needs, and their expectations are determined and measured

- How the organization's processes are designed to meet the customer's needs and expectations

- How the organization's processes are organized to ensure an uninterrupted flow of information and material from suppliers to customers

- How the organization ensures that the methods and tools used in the processes are available when they are needed and capable of performing the requirements of the work

- How the organization ensures that its people have the right skills and understand how to do their work

- How the organization takes into consideration individual knowledge, skills, and capabilities when building teams

- How the organization creates an environment conducive to the success of each person, individually and as a member of a team

- How the organization ensures the engagement of suppliers as an integral part of the organization's processes

- How the organization supports a continuous improvement culture by providing a common set of processes, tools, and methods for improvement work

The assessment questions are intended to discover opportunities for improvement in three basic areas. These areas were originally defined through the Baldrige National Quality Award Criteria. They include:

- What is the approach? Has the process been defined and documented?

- Has the process been deployed? Are those for whom it is intended following the defined process?

- Are the customer's and organization's results world-class? Can the organization show that the processes used drive their results to world-class levels? How do results compare to the competition and best-in-class organizations?

The assessment is conducted with different people from across the processes:

- **Customers.** What do customers think about the products and services of the process and/or the organization? Are the customers' needs being met? How well are the customers' needs being met? How does the organization work with the customers to understand their needs?

- **The people doing the work.** What problems do the people see? How can the work be done better? What are the things that get in the way of world-class performance?

- **Suppliers.** How are suppliers integrated with the work of the process? How are requirements identified and communicated to the suppliers? What do the suppliers measure and how is that connected to the processes they supply?

- **Process management and leadership.** How does leadership think things are going? What does leadership pay attention to? How does leadership determine if things are working as they should? How does leadership ensure that the customers and suppliers are integrated with the organization's processes?

Following the collection of information during the assessment process, a set of improvement priorities are delivered in the form of a feedback report. The feedback report can be created using a variety of approaches. (Baldrige assessor training is a good source for how to determine and prepare feedback) One approach that can be used for feedback development is the following:

- Construct an affinity diagram or KJ from the individual elements of information to determine different categories of improvement.

- Use a priority (C&E) matrix to identify priorities relative to the organization's goals and strategies.

- Determine the three to five most important improvement areas and develop a feedback report discussing these areas and any recommendations for improvement that apply.

A healthy organization sees problems and performance gaps as an opportunity to make things better for customers and other users of its products and services. A continuous assessment attitude is a key element of a continuous improvement culture

14

A Continuously Improving Continuous Improvement Culture

As discussed in the previous chapter, Toyota is a company known for quality. It has created a quality-focused organization by staying true to the philosophy that finding and fixing problems is a good thing for the company to do. An appropriate mantra is "We want to see our problems." By finding and fixing problems throughout the organization, Toyota has continuously improved its products and consistently ranked highest in customer-experienced quality. This attitude exists at all levels of the organization (Liker, 2003).

One may ask what happened to the quality of Toyota products during an approximately five-year period in the early 2000s. This was a period during which safety and other product-quality problems dominated the news about the company. In a 2010 statement to the United States Congress Toyota President Akio Toyoda said the following regarding Toyota's quality problems:

> Toyota has, for the past few years, been expanding its business rapidly. Quite frankly, I fear the pace at which we have grown may have been too quick. I would like to point out here that Toyota's priority has traditionally been the following: First, Safety; Second, Quality; and Third, Volume. These priorities became confused, and we were not able to stop, think, and make improvements as much as we were able to before, and our basic stance to listen to customers' voices to make better products has weakened somewhat. We pursued growth over the speed at which we were able to develop our people and our organization, and we should sincerely be mindful of that. I regret that this has resulted in the safety issues described in the recalls we face today, and I am deeply sorry for any accidents that Toyota drivers have experienced.

Other research supports this admission. It was a leadership decision that caused Toyota's problems. The desire to become the world's largest car company replaced their traditional goals of safety and quality first. As Toyota returned to their traditional priorities, products rapidly returned to previous quality levels as reflected in their ratings in many quality-oriented publications, surveys, and reports.

The advantage that Toyota has over many other organizations is that the company was founded under the principle that safety and quality are most important. It has built a continuous improvement culture over many decades. This culture has become a key component of how the company is led and managed. But, as the previous example shows, this focus is all too easily lost if the leadership is not constantly diligent regarding the stewardship of the organization's priorities and the way they are communicated.

Most organizations don't start this way. Companies begin with a product or service to sell. The company works to attract customers, hires people to meet the demands of those customers, and spends capital as those demands increase. Generally, the early focus of management is on survival and growth. Developing a company culture and determining a philosophy and vision generally evolve with time as the organization stabilizes and moves out of survival mode. Unfortunately, by the time the organization gets around to creating these cultural definitions, many patterns of behavior are already well ingrained. If an organization wasn't built with continuous improvement as a foundation, developing a culture of continuous improvement and changing entrenched behaviors requires a huge change effort.

THE IMPORTANCE OF A CONTINUOUS IMPROVEMENT CULTURE

A continuous improvement culture is important because perfection is impossible. The product or service is used in unexpected ways. Suppliers to the organization change or increase, creating variation in the supplies received. The employee base expands and changes, creating a new source of variation in how people make the products and services delivered. Technology changes and in turn changes the processes used to produce the products or services offered by the organization. The customer base changes as it grows. Customer expectations change as new customers and users develop. Customers and users also become more demanding with time as their expectations for how the product or service performs increase (see the Kano Model). All of this variation drives a need for continuous improvement of everything that the organization does, because variation is the enemy of perceived and real product and service quality. When things change in an uncontrolled way problems occur. These problems ultimately affect customers. Maintaining the status quo is not an option for an organization that wants to grow. Developing a continuous improvement culture that sees every problem as an opportunity to better meet customer and user expectations is a key element of organizational survival and growth.

Changing to a continuous improvement culture is as difficult as any other change and requires all of the change processes that have been discussed in this book. In an organization lacking a continuous improvement culture and approach, problems are addressed in an uncoordinated way as individual events.

All organizations are complex. The processes of an organization are interwoven and dependent on one another for delivering the organization's products and services. Behaving as if problems are unexpected surprises that call for emergency action introduces an entirely new level of variation that conflicts with the organization's main goal of delivering its products and services to customers and users. A continuous improvement approach that is the organization's common language, commonly applied and enforced, enables an organization to coordinate improvements based on the needs of all stakeholders, including customers, suppliers, and the organization's members.

The process of changing to a culture of continuous improvement faces many challenges. Common challenges include:

* Time

* Discipline

* Resources

* Organizational size

Change Takes Time

As discussed earlier, organizational leadership tends to be impatient for results. For example, in publicly-held companies, the pressure for quarter-to-quarter results is relentless. This pressure can tend to create an attitude that values immediate over long-term results. Many leaders move up the ranks because of the short-term results they produced in different roles. This creates results-driven management teams that place a premium on the short term.

In a complex organization, structural and cultural change takes a significant amount of time. Simply communicating to a complex organization's people is a challenge. It almost goes without saying that changing behavior and attitudes takes much longer. Leadership commitment is necessary because, while continuing to produce short-term results, the long-term changes to a continuously improving organization have to be viewed as valuable because of their impact to both the organization's customers and results. This commitment ensures that the time and political protection needed for the change to be successfully implemented is provided. It is important to keep the short- and long-term priorities in balance.

Change Takes Discipline

A disciplined approach to organizational change means deciding what the future state of the organization looks like and sticking with it long enough to bring the change to fruition. There will be ups and downs over the course of changing to a continuous improvement culture. Because it takes time, there will be management changes and business/organization cycles. Staying disciplined through these cyclical realities is a key to a successful change to a continuous improvement culture.

Change Costs Money and the Return Is Frequently Delayed

The costs of change are numerous. Training, consultants, reviews, projects, hiring people with new skills, new equipment; the costs go on and on. Because of the time involved, the return on investment (ROI) has to be seen as part of a long-term investment in future success. This delay reinforces the need for the long view and the discipline to see it through.

The Bigger the Organization, the More People Need to Be Enrolled in the Practice of Continuous Improvement

The greatest potential value comes from comprehensive continuous improvement across the whole organization. Improvements in the hand-offs between processes owned by headquarters, operating units, and individual locations are difficult to identify and even more difficult to improve because they require unselfish cooperation between internal organizations. This implies that the language of improvement has been widely shared and practiced. Of course, the larger and more far-flung the organization, the more difficult this task becomes. Its difficulty, however, makes it no less important.

It doesn't matter which approach is chosen. Today there are many approaches available for the work of continuous improvement. Lean, Six Sigma, Lean Six Sigma, Shanin Red X, Seven Step Problem Solving, Plan-Do-Check-Act (PDCA), and Ford 8-D are among the recognized approaches to problem solving and continuous improvement. The truth is that they all work and they are all difficult to implement successfully. My overall recommendation is to just pick one. My specific recommendation is that Lean Six Sigma is the best of the bunch based on both my personal experience and research into the others. In the work that I have done and experienced during 20-plus years in the field, I have come to the conclusion that Lean Six Sigma is the most flexible for solving problems and continuous improvement of processes that we currently have available. It incorporates the best of all the processes in a way that delivers a consistently high-quality result in quantifiable business terms. It is also the hardest of the processes to implement. However, regardless of the approach chosen, success is about choice and discipline.

The key first step is to begin. In the end, I believe one should apply this quote from General George S. Patton, "I would rather have a good plan today than a perfect plan two weeks from now." Research and pick an approach best matched to the needs and culture of your organization as discussed in earlier chapters. Develop a plan. And then, execute, execute, execute.

The reason this is important for conversion to a continuous improvement culture is that organizations are not naturally inclined toward this work. An organization is set up for the delivery of a product and/or service. Continuous improvement can appear easy in one sense and a distraction in another. To make this change requires commitment, resources, and time. Committing to a specific philosophy and process gives the work a direction and results are measurable over time.

The basic continuous improvement process has been defined over the last hundred years. This process (Figure 14.1) is a repeating cycle and contains the following elements.

Stakeholder Voices

The voices of technology (VOT), the customer (VOC), the business (VOB), and everything else that matters (VOE) are the starting points for continuous improvement. These voices collectively define the

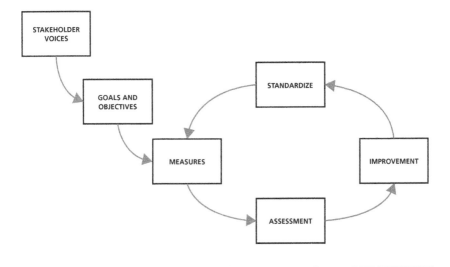

Figure 14.1 The continuous improvement cycle.

requirements and needs of the users of the organization's products and services. Knowing these requirements and interpreting them in relation to the organization's products and services provides a focus for improvement.

Goals and Objectives

Having identified needs and requirements, goals and objectives are established to drive the organization to make improvements (including new products or services) that are designed to meet these needs and requirements.

Measurement

Progress toward goals and objectives is monitored to determine if actual progress is being made. Progress is monitored through the use of specific measures. As often as possible, these measures are quantifiable and best seen as trends over time. Examples of measurements are on-time delivery, customer-experienced defects, new product development effectiveness, profitability, market share, and responsiveness to customer problems. These measures should reflect the needs and priorities of both customers and the organization. Additionally, these measures can be compared to the industry or best in class to determine where competitive improvement is necessary.

Assessment

Assessment is a continuous activity used as a tool by management to identify needed improvements in the processes. Toyota is built on a philosophy of "wanting to see our problems." A practical way to practice this philosophy is the use of systematic assessment to identify the organization's problems.

Improvement

Once problems are identified, improvement actions follow. There are many ways to improve. Using Lean Six Sigma to improve is one of the more effective approaches.

Standardize

Following improvement, the result is made permanent so that the problem doesn't recur. Developing fail-safes, training, process ownership, and developing policies and procedures singly or in combination is the work of standardization.

Continuous improvement is one of the cornerstones of growing and maturing an organization. It is the job of leadership to establish this cornerstone.

15

One Company's Experience Creating a Continuous Improvement Culture

As earlier stated, I spent 16 years deploying Six Sigma at Cummins, Inc., ultimately evolving into a version of Lean Six Sigma. This chapter addresses why I believe Lean Six Sigma to be the best approach available today for creating a continuous improvement culture.

Lean Six Sigma is an excellent improvement process, but it's not the only one. The last half of the 20th century saw the rise of various problem solving and continuous improvement methodologies within the professional quality community. I have tried several of these processes, and while all are useful if practiced with discipline and consistency, I have found Lean Six Sigma to be the most powerful.

The magic of Lean Six Sigma comes from linking statistical tools and other concepts. Prior to Lean Six Sigma, each of the quality tools tended to be used independently. Their use would reveal information about a problem or a process, but lacked the ability to fully reveal the true causes. Motorola's quality professionals and statisticians discovered connections between the various tools that previously hadn't been noticed and developed them into a repeatable system. The connections through the phases of this system, Define-Measure-Analyze-Improve-Control, yielded a clearly defined, controllable result. Motorola, GE, Allied Signal, and a few others developed, improved, and matured the process. Companies like Cummins, DuPont, Dow, and others built on that legacy, making Lean Six Sigma a key element in how the organizations worked and delivered products and services to their customers.

WHY IT WORKS

As previously mentioned, the magic is the linkage of tools together for the purpose of elegantly and efficiently finding the most important causes of waste and variation in processes. This waste and variation is why problems occur. This idea is central to every good problem solving or continuous improvement methodology.

All results come from processes. These processes are designed to deliver the result perfectly every time. Nobody designs a process to fail 10 percent or 25 percent of the time. So, what happens? Something changes in the process to alter the output. The "something changed" is variation and/or waste. Lean Six Sigma is uniquely designed to find that variation and waste so that improvements can be made to eliminate it.

It is important to understand that variation and waste are the enemies of quality. Variation and waste are the reason why customers of the organization receive products and services that don't meet their needs and requirements, which causes problems. Lean Six Sigma works because the leadership of the organization recognizes this truth about waste and variation and understands its responsibility to continuously improve the products and services for the organization's customers. The leadership is, therefore, willing to invest resources and management capital to drive out waste and variation because of its impact on product and service quality. It is this leadership discipline and focus that allows Lean Six Sigma to succeed. It is hard work and requires a perseverance that is critical and very difficult for most leadership teams to sustain over the necessary time required for success.

HOW IT WORKS

Define-Measure-Analyze-Improve-Control (DMAIC) is the Six Sigma process. It is a logic trail that one follows when continuously improving processes or solving problems. The logic applies anytime there is a question or a problem that can't be easily answered or solved. Six Sigma is not just about statistics; it is about a logical approach. But, when the data is available, there are very effective and powerful statistical tools that can be used to understand what the data is saying about the problem's causes.

Key to how Lean Six Sigma works is the people in the organization who, over time, come to understand the value of data-based decision making. All processes are spewing data. We just don't take the time to develop collection systems for gathering up data. Lean Six Sigma teaches people the value of collecting the data and using statistical and non-statistical tools to understand what the data are telling us. This is the voice of the process. The voice of the process is the story that the process's data are telling. The statistical tools help put that story together. When the products and services of the organization are failing to meet the needs and requirements of the customers, the voice of the process tells leadership why. The mature leadership team wants to see the organization's problems and sees Lean Six Sigma as a process and set of tools for elegantly and efficiently addressing them.

HOW TO GET THE MOST OUT OF IT

Lean Six Sigma is not something that the typical organization can develop on its own. The methodology is stable and well-defined. Further, there are some technical components that are standard and difficult to create. Hiring a consultant to get started is the quickest and surest way to begin seeing results as rapidly as possible. However, make sure to contractually establish authorization for use of the consultant's intellectual property. It is also important to define an end point for the consultant by specifying a date of termination. This provides the organization with a sense of urgency to understand and own the process internally. This commitment to own the process is important for making continuous improvement a business imperative that goes far beyond the simple training of tools.

The elements of successful organizational application include understanding that Lean Six Sigma is results-driven training. First, there is no "sheep-dipping" in Lean Six Sigma. By this I mean Lean Six Sigma training is not universal training for training's sake. Nobody attends training without a project. NOBODY! This is not a training program. It is a business tool. Project completion and a tangible return on the training investment is an expectation of training attendance.

Each project is expected to deliver real, measureable improvement. This improvement is most often measured in cost savings. I have seen organizations do this in different ways and I don't believe there is one right answer. But the improvement and savings have to be real and a central part of the project. Results capture leadership's attention and are therefore critical to sustained success of Lean Six Sigma. How these savings are recorded and captured is a matter of organizational structure and culture. Therefore, how to capture and record savings is a decision for the organization to make. There are a number of books and websites with this information available.

Pick the best people in the organization to be the initial project leaders (*Belts* in the language of Lean Six Sigma). This is always difficult to do, but sets the premise that finding and fixing problems is important work and must be resourced to reflect this intent. Therefore, this work requires the organization's best people.

Involving leadership is not a passive activity. The best organization's leaders learn the process and lead projects. This serves as an example for those in the organization and helps the leaders understand the value of the process at a deeper level. Leaders can also be sponsors/champions of projects and perform as team members. Early in the process, senior executive leadership's review of individual projects tells the organization that Six Sigma is more than training; it is something that is important for success. The bottom line is that the organization's leadership is spending management capital on one of its critical priorities and the organization sees that.

Project selection and control plan review processes are two keys to success. In the early stages of a Six Sigma deployment, the emphasis is on learning what it is, seeing if it really works, and working with the consultant. Two important elements often forgotten or ignored are defining a project selection process and a control plan review process. It is natural to forget these two processes because in the beginning of Six Sigma, almost any project produces a result. The development of control plans is so far away that the assumption is "we will get to it." However, developing processes for project selection and control plan review can be difficult to do later in the effort. Often, random selection of projects is established early as a precedent and becomes standard practice and difficult to change. Control plan reviews and audits seem unnecessary in the early days because few projects are closed. There is so much attention paid to each individual project that a review and audit process seems unnecessary. As Lean Six Sigma accelerates over time, selection of good projects becomes more difficult and the pile of control plans becomes unmanageable one plan at a time.

A good project selection process is one that connects each project to the goals, strategies, and initiatives of the organization. We discussed Goal Trees earlier. Each critical project should find its way onto the organization's Goal Tree cascade. Having a process that assesses current organizational performance using customer and organizational health metrics along with process assessment results are the keys to the identification of continuous improvement opportunities. As Lean Six Sigma matures, the project selection process includes customers, suppliers, and other internal sub-units and functions that depend on one another for the development and delivery of the organization's products and services across its supply chains.

Control plan audits and reviews are an essential aspect of the control phase of DMAIC Lean Six Sigma. Each project produces a control plan defining the actions the process owner is to take to ensure the improvement becomes a permanent part of the process. Lacking a robust audit and review process, these control plans tend to get lost in the day-to-day activities of the organization. It isn't always simply because people aren't interested. It is, for the most part, because this is new work in the organization. It is change. For change to become established as normal work takes time, attention, and correction. The control plan audit and review process is intended to make control plans part of normal work and important to the overall workings of the organization.

Continuous improvement is synonymous with change and is a main leadership job. We have discussed S-Curves and organizational maturity. For the organization to mature, it has to be led by leadership. This is not something extra. Leadership of a change cannot be delegated. The change is a part of the standard work plan for leaders of the organization. It is on the CEO's work plan. The change is on the work plans of the senior executive leadership team. It is the focus of the planning process. The change is clearly spelled out in organization Goal Trees and other planning documents. Management capital is spent leading, coaching, engaging in, and managing the change. Absent this effort and focus, broad organizational changes fail to produce the intended results. This is a simple fact often misunderstood by organizational leadership. It is difficult and time consuming, but a necessity nonetheless.

16

Final Comments

Having discussed the particulars, both good and bad, of change in complex organizations, I will wrap-up with a possible road map for successful change. Remember, the basic goal is to systematically change the behavior of an organization. The approaches described can be applied to any complex organization, regardless of size.

Like everything else, this is a process. The following describes a proposed path for making systematic organizational change.

First, the change has to be leadership's idea. The idea of change can come from the main leader or the leadership team depending on the culture of the company. The idea can come from one of many sources. Some examples include:

- Other senior executive leaders of organizations. It's said that the only person that understands the trials and tribulations of the President of the United States is another President of the United States. It is a very exclusive club. The same is true of any organization leader. Others don't have the same view. Ideas coming from other leaders with similar pressures carry significant weight.

- Trusted subordinates are a good source of ideas. However, my experience is that senior executive leadership has a hard time hearing this group. I'm not exactly sure why this is true and I'm sure it is not true everywhere, but it has been my experience that ideas bubbling up from inside the complex organization are often discounted. However, having said that, if the internal source is someone who is trusted by the senior executive leadership, this can be a good source of new ideas.

- Consultants can be a good source of new ideas for senior executive leadership. The reception is based on a combination of the organization's culture and the quality of the consultant.

- Books are another source, but seem to be less influential than in times past.

The bottom line is that the leadership must own the idea regardless of where it comes from. The leadership must also think it is important to the future of the organization and its customers, and personally commit to the implementation of the change. This is the first, most important step to success.

The leadership describes what the future holds based on what they have seen and what they want for their organization. This future state is a picture of what the organization will be and how it will be better. This gives the organization a direction and a focus for continuous improvement.

Next, an operational leader is selected who will drive the day-to-day details. This person is somebody who is trusted and is selected by leadership specifically for the job. This person has credibility across the organization and is well known for getting things done.

The search is then made for a ready-made package of communication, education, and training for the change. The organization owns deployment, but buys the process because it saves time and leverages already tried and tested approaches. If consultants are used for initial teaching and system set-up, the contract specifies that they depart at a pre-determined date leaving behind intellectual property and organizational capability to continue deployment. This reinforces the need for local organizations to accept accountability for the change.

Some other steps include:

- Establish business measures of success. The more closely tied to customer and organizational success measures the change is, the quicker real and believable improvement can be seen.

- Establish scorecards that relate to the activities that must be accomplished as part of the maturation of the change. Scorecards change over time and are connected to each S-Curve of change related to the future state.

Leadership devotes time to learn and use the change. This shows people in the organization that the change is not optional.

Leadership is patient but doesn't tolerate resistance from other organization leaders. Time is given to learn what the change is and how to apply it, but there is a time when subordinate leaders have to decide whether to become part of the change or to leave the organization. There cannot be room for those who will not accept the change. If there are leaders who will not adopt the change, what other policies are they ignoring? They are poor examples and need to find someplace else to work.

Leadership is accountable for ongoing review of the progress made and identification of the best practices. This reinforces the change, gives the leadership a realistic picture of how things are going, and allows for important, real-time course corrections.

Finally, persistence is key. In a complex organization, change takes time. It always takes more time than the leadership desires. Changing the behavior of people is no easy task. A combination of all of the above factors reinforces persistence and creates a fertile environment for realizing the full impacts of a system-wide change.

I wrote this book to capture lessons that I have learned during my career. They are not absolutes. My intent was to write it so that there would be something that any leader could learn and apply to their organization.

Thank you for taking the time to read it and I hope it has been helpful.

Bibliography

Adams, Jonathan. *North America During the Last 150,000 Years.* Oak Ridge, TN: Environmental Sciences Division, Oak Ridge National Laboratory, 1997.

Anand, Gopesh, Peter T. Ward, Mohan V. Tatikonda, and David A. Schilling. "Dynamic Capabilities Through Continuous Improvement Infrastructure," *Journal of Operations Management,* vol. 27, no. 6 (2009): 444–461.

Baldrige National Quality Award Program, Criteria for Performance Excellence.

Brassard, Michael. *The Memory Jogger Plus — The Seven Management Planning Tools.* Methuen, MA: Goal QPC, 1996.

Kamen, Dean, "Dark Night of the Innovator." Speech, September 24, 2003, at the LaCentre Conference Center, Westlake, Ohio.

Liker, Jeffery. *The Toyota Way: 14 Management Principles From the World's Greatest Manufacturer.* New York: McGraw Hill Education, 2011.

Morris, Betsy. "New Rule: Look Out, Not In: Old Rule: Be Lean and Mean." *Fortune* (July 11, 2006).

Peter, Laurence J., and Raymond Hull, *The Peter Principle: Why Things Always Go Wrong.* New York: William and Morrow, 1969.

TRIZ—Processes and Tools Accessible from PQR Group, Upland, California.

Miller, Christopher W., *A Workbook for Innovation: Developing New Product Concepts.* Lancaster, PA: Innovation Focus Inc., 2004.

References

[i] Betsy Morris, "New Rule: Look Out, Not In. Old rule: Be Lean and Mean," *Fortune Magazine*, July 11, 2006. http://archive.fortune.com/2006/07/10/magazines/fortune/rule4.fortune/index.htm

[ii] Christopher Miller, *Developing New Product Concepts: A Workbook For Innovation*, (Lancaster, PA: Innovation Focus Inc., 2004).

Index

The Knowledge Center
www.asq.org/knowledge-center

Learn about quality. Apply it. Share it.

ASQ's online Knowledge Center is the place to:

- Stay on top of the latest in quality with Editor's Picks and Hot Topics.

- Search ASQ's collection of articles, books, tools, training, and more.

- Connect with ASQ staff for personalized help hunting down the knowledge you need, the networking opportunities that will keep your career and organization moving forward, and the publishing opportunities that are the best fit for you.

Use the Knowledge Center Search to quickly sort through hundreds of books, articles, and other software-related publications.

www.asq.org/knowledge-center

TRAINING CERTIFICATION CONFERENCES MEMBERSHIP **PUBLICATIONS**   The Global Voice of Quality®

Ask a Librarian

<u>Did you know?</u>

- The ASQ Quality Information Center contains a wealth of knowledge and information available to ASQ members and non-members

- A librarian is available to answer research requests using ASQ's ever-expanding library of relevant, credible quality resources, including journals, conference proceedings, case studies and Quality Press publications

- ASQ members receive free internal information searches and reduced rates for article purchases

- You can also contact the Quality Information Center to request permission to reuse or reprint ASQ copyrighted material, including journal articles and book excerpts

- For more information or to submit a question, visit **http://asq.org/knowledge-center/ask-a-librarian-index**

Visit **www.asq.org/qic for more information.**

ASQ
The Global Voice of Quality®

Belong to the Quality Community!

Established in 1946, ASQ is a global community of quality experts in all fields and industries. ASQ is dedicated to the promotion and advancement of quality tools, principles, and practices in the workplace and in the community.

The Society also serves as an advocate for quality. Its members have informed and advised the U.S. Congress, government agencies, state legislatures, and other groups and individuals worldwide on quality-related topics.

Vision

By making quality a global priority, an organizational imperative, and a personal ethic, ASQ becomes the community of choice for everyone who seeks quality technology, concepts, or tools to improve themselves and their world.

ASQ is...

- More than 90,000 individuals and 700 companies in more than 100 countries

- The world's largest organization dedicated to promoting quality

- A community of professionals striving to bring quality to their work and their lives

- The administrator of the Malcolm Baldrige National Quality Award

- A supporter of quality in all sectors including manufacturing, service, healthcare, government, and education

- YOU

Visit www.asq.org for more information.

TRAINING CERTIFICATION CONFERENCES MEMBERSHIP **PUBLICATIONS**

ASQ Membership

Research shows that people who join associations experience increased job satisfaction, earn more, and are generally happier*. ASQ membership can help you achieve this while providing the tools you need to be successful in your industry and to distinguish yourself from your competition. So why wouldn't you want to be a part of ASQ?

Networking

Have the opportunity to meet, communicate, and collaborate with your peers within the quality community through conferences and local ASQ section meetings, ASQ forums or divisions, ASQ Communities of Quality discussion boards, and more.

Professional Development

Access a wide variety of professional development tools such as books, training, and certifications at a discounted price. Also, ASQ certifications and the ASQ Career Center help enhance your quality knowledge and take your career to the next level.

Solutions

Find answers to all your quality problems, big and small, with ASQ's Knowledge Center, mentoring program, various e-newsletters, *Quality Progress* magazine, and industry-specific products.

Access to Information

Learn classic and current quality principles and theories in ASQ's Quality Information Center (QIC), *ASQ Weekly* e-newsletter, and product offerings.

Advocacy Programs

ASQ helps create a better community, government, and world through initiatives that include social responsibility, Washington advocacy, and Community Good Works.

Visit www.asq.org/membership for more information on ASQ membership.

*2008, The William E. Smith Institute for Association Research

TRAINING CERTIFICATION CONFERENCES **MEMBERSHIP PUBLICATIONS**

The Global Voice of Quality®